WITHDRAWN

10-13

REVOLUTIONARY ACTIONS . . . U.S.A. . . .

In Retrospect

What To Do Now

Compiled by

BRUCE ALGER

With a Brief

DICTIONARY OF DOUBLE TALK

Socialist/Communese-English

by

ROY E. COLBY

Published by

THE CITIZENS EVALUATION INSTITUTE

TABLE OF CONTENTS
PART ONE
REVOLUTIONARY ACTIONS. . . U.S.A. . . .
Compiled by Bruce Alger

PART TWO
A BRIEF DICTIONARY OF DOUBLE TALK
Socialist/Communese-English
By Roy E. Colby

PART THREE
APPENDIX
Campus Speakers and Honoraria
From Report, Committee on Internal Security,
House of Representatives

PART I

REVOLUTIONARY ACTIONS . . . U.S.A.

. . . Just as the Ten Commandments and the Golden Rule came down through the ages as basic, moral fundamentals to be obeyed if man is to live with man in a social order, so have certain basic economic fundamentals come down to us. These must be observed if man is to improve his lot materially above the bare subsistence level and pre-serve his human freedom. The moral funda-mentals of the Ten Commandments and the eco-nomic fundamentals—which are called 'Natural Economic Laws'—are inherent in our Constitution. They are responsible for the miracle which is the United States of America, and which in less than 200 years catapulted its people to heights never before achieved by any previous social order—nor by any since.

However, increasingly today, we are being told that these fundamental moral and economic laws are no longer appropriate and must be modified or discarded. Many government officials, educators, clergymen and businessmen have been taken in by this line. Today, about half of the population of this country is 25 years of age or under. This means that the present younger generation will either carry on the heritage and tradition of this wonderful and unique system of free enterprise, which is based on individual freedom, or will scuttle it, possibly unwittingly, in favor of a collec-tive, regulated, totalitarian system. If the latter, then all of us, young and old, will have little, if any, individual freedom. . . .

WARREN T. HACKETT
in *How We Prosper Under Freedom*

Briefly about
The Honorable Bruce Alger

Mr. Alger is a member, Board of Directors, CITIZENS EVALUATION INSTITUTE. He served ten years in the U.S. House of Representatives as Congressman from Dallas County, Texas. He is an eloquent speaker and lecturer.

He served on the important Ways and Means Committee, the Public Works Committee and the Interstate and Foreign Commerce Committee. He always used two yardsticks when evaluating proposed legislation ... *Is it a function of Federal Government? Can we afford it?* He consistently earned a 100% Americans for Constitutional Action voting record.

He served as Chairman of the Prayer Group in the House. He also served on the Committee to Study the Effect of Government Programs on the Free Enterprise System and sponsored legislation embodying the Hoover Commission Recommendations.

Mr. Alger is a devoted student of the libertarian philosophy. He is firm in his convictions that the Scriptures are the source of the moral underpinning of a Free Society.

He is an ardent advocate of a healthy body and a clean mind. He actively participated in athletics in high school and college and played on the Princeton championship football and track teams and is a former handball doubles champion.

He has been active in civic affairs, Chamber of Commerce work and Kiwanian activities and is a Bible student.

His studies convince him that the Ten Commandments and the Sermon on the Mount are revered by Christians whose personal Savior is Christ and respected by non-Christians who have not yet acknowledged Him as his or her personal Savior.

Mr. Alger served as a B-29 Commander in World War II and holds the Distinguished Flying Cross and Air Medal with clusters. He is presently in the real estate business in Florida.

INTRODUCTION

Bruce Alger

Having softened up the general attitude of the public by violence and generated a feeling of fear, the Marxist-Socialists, their advocates and followers can be expected to shift tactics in 1971 and 1972.

After all, 1972 is an important election year. Preparation to win will be made by the candidates beginning in 1971.

The more astute planners for political victories realize that the American people abhor violence. They know that most voters want law and order with justice.

Hence, a common denominator of most campaigns will be "peaceful change." Some will want "change" faster than others. Some will want more change, others less.

But the illusion will be created and used persistently that *any change*, regardless of consequences—if peaceful—and if it is secured democratically — *change is perfectly all right.*

In the political processes, an effort will be made to disown radical revolutionaries. The politician will attempt to disassociate himself from the Jerry Rubins, the Kunstlers, the Rap Browns, the Angela Davises, the Panthers—some may even disown some Socialist teachers and some radical college presidents—if they appear to be a political liability. But they will be supporting the goals behind the scenes.

NEW 'NON-VIOLENCE' WITH 'NEW' POLITICS

The following case illustrates the point.

On the weekend of February 20, 1971, students and other radicals from over 30 states gathered at Catholic University in Washington, D.C.

The purpose was to plan more nation-wide anti-war demonstrations throughout the U.S. . . . to rock our foundations.

The host was the Student Mobilization Committee, working with the *new* National Peace Action Committee. But the groups behind it and involved are not new. They included the Young Socialist Alliance, the Socialist Workers Parties, the National Caucus of Labor Committees, Angela Davis Defense Committee, G.I.'s United Against the War, Chicano Mobilization Committee, the League of Arab States Information and others.

While it is hard to understand how respectable citizens will support such groups, knowing the real goals of those behind them, a few liberals, including past and present public officials and politicians will do so — they will hide it by identifying with the *new* peaceful front.

The Washington Post, February 20, 1971, reported that a representative of Female Liberation said they should join the anti-war movement but "we will not become movement bunnies."

GOALS REMAIN THE SAME

Of paramount importance to the American people, however, is that we all understand a single central fact:

> *The goals of the Marxist-Socialists and their advocates and followers remain the same . . . change America into a complete Socialist State.*

LOCAL GOVERNMENTS ARE TARGETS

But the more impressive targets of the so-called political (peaceful) revolution is the capture and control of cities or of their parts, if not all of some of their operating departments.

Dr. George S. Benson, former President of Harding College (Ark.) and now President of the American Heritage Center, describes one such effort.

In his National Program Letter, he reports:

RADICALS 'STACK THE DECK' AT BERKELEY

". . . THE DAILY CALIFORNIAN, student newspaper of the University of California at Berkeley, which serves its 27,000 students, several thousand faculty, perhaps 10,000 'street people,' and a large segment of the Negro community

of Berkeley, has become a powerful voice for the radical
political coalition which seeks, with the Black Panther
Party and the "National Committees to Combat Fascism,"
to take over control of the city and its institutions. A
January 8 editorial urged that the radical elements: 'Seize
the City!' The editorial said: 'The April 6 Movement, a
campus organization . . . has undertaken the task of regis-
tering 10,000 voters before the deadline (April 6 city elections), and time is running out. Go to the table at Sather
Gate (historic University entrance) to register and volunteer to help . . . The NCCF Community Control of
Police measure will be on the ballot, along with four City
Council spots and the mayor's office. The present Council
and Mayor are scared . . . Too late . . . We want the city
and we want it now!'

The present government of the city of Berkeley is indeed frightened. The non-radical citizens of Berkeley are
frightened. If the University radicals register 10,000
student-and-faculty voters in addition to present registra-
tions, and if the Panthers and their comrades get the
potential radical vote to the polls, they can take over the
city legally. Should they bring it off, some of the best
informed citizen leaders in Berkeley say the city soon
would have "a form of Marxist-Maoist" control.

PADDING THE VOTE ROLLS

"As of October 14, 1970, there were 75,269 registered
voters in the city of 113,000. This is the highest ratio of
voters to population in the country. The reason for the
record is that hippies, 'street people' and radical tran-
sients of all descriptions, with just 90 days residence in
Berkeley, can register and vote. Among the 75,269 are
51,269 declared Democrats, 15,550 Republicans, 3,151
Peace and Freedom Party members and about 5,055 frag-
mented and 'party not stated.' The voting situation for one
of the most important city elections in American history is
fantastic, virtually "out of control."

MASS REGISTRATIONS

"It has worsened even since the November elections,
when Ed Montgomery, top subversive activities reporter of

the *San Francisco Chronicle,* wrote: "Alameda County (Berkeley-Oakland) District Attorney Lowell Jansen and Edith Campbell, Berkeley City Clerk, agree that as the election code now stands interpreted it theoretically would be possible for 20,000 hippies, say, to converge on Berkeley, register 90 days in advance of an election, from any address bona fide or otherwise, and seize control of the city government in any given election." Theoretically? It *is* happening now! . . ."

SOCIALISM BY A NEW NAME

The names given to the resulting system for propaganda purposes, will, in the interim, vary. Some may call it "Democratic Socialism." Others may say they seek an "Effective Government"—or a "Government that Cares"—or a "Problem Solving Government"—or a "Liberal Government"—or a "Government that Really Works." Some, to gather support from the conservative elements, will "just want to make real the intentions of the Founding Fathers."

But "CHANGE," "peaceful *change*" or "revolutionary peaceful change" will be watchwords for the process.

A Socialist America, however, will remain the real goal.

TACTICS AND STRATEGY WILL SHIFT

To achieve their ends, at least three shifts in means—tactics—are clearly evident.

One will be a shift to: *Political* methods—rather than extensive use of violent confrontation.

Since the media and other opinion molders will emphasize "peaceful change" to "cure the faults of our system" by "democratic processes," the "New Left" and the "Old Left" will join hands to secure all kinds of new social programs and enlarge present ones. They will seek to elect candidates who promise to push for more programs "for the poor, minorities, the elderly, the sick, the cities, the farmers and the schools," and seek bigger appropriations for them.

These people and institutions have problems. So have others. The real ones should be recognized. The fallacy that bigger government, with more Socialistic programs can solve them, should be well understood. After centuries of trying to solve them by governments it should be clear that governments cannot solve them and still permit maximum individual freedom.

Double talk semantics will be artfully employed. For instance, "relief for the over-burdened taxpayer" will be high on the list (while slyly calling for more tax money). The idealistic youths, whether they vote or not, will be appealed "to work for the improvement of the system." Churches and political parties can be expected to be allied in the drive for "peaceful change."

BOMB AND BURN SELECTIVELY

The second shift of tactics will be to *bomb*, or *burn, selected targets*—rather than directly cause widespread promiscuous destruction.

These targets will be directed to disturb the "power structure in the establishment."

Banks, office buildings, low-cost housing units, homes of key officials, tunnels, courthouses, key government buildings . . . even churches and schools . . . appear to be examples. Brief advance notice will be given . . . some as threats to create fear, while others will actually be carried out.

Kidnapping and blackmail of key people—in government, as well as in business and industry—is also a part of the arsenal of shifted techniques, as J. Edgar Hoover has warned.

These terror techniques will be carried out by militant fronts for existing groups, or by those whose innocence seems so obvious that guilt will be difficult for the public to believe. "A conspiracy of conscience" has already been asserted as a defense.

Terrorists will find well-financed legal shelter from attorneys who have or are making a career of defending anarchists of all kinds.

Many of the terrorists will be excused under the umbrella label as being "civil libertarians." The true libertarian philosophy—which is linked to personal responsibility, a high moral order, belief in God, and basic limited constitutional functions of government, is being purposely misread and misinterpreted. This is calculated to somehow mislead those who believe in true libertarianism defined by Bastiat, and Ludwig Von Mises, and made popular by Leonard Read and others. Such misinterpretation may secure acquiesence by responsible people for their foul deeds and causes.

The third shift in tactics will probably be to *play down the frontal attack on business and everything capitalistic*.

Instead, while not accepting American capitalism, the "System" and capitalism will continue to be labeled "immoral" or at least immoral as "it now operates." The rhetoric will call for "changes that make it moral," or change "capitalism so all will share and participate."

The drive will be for more government controls while calling for more "freedom," cutting appropriations for all forms of military security and preparedness (some wars are immoral, you know), for more restrictions on the Federal Bureau of Investigation and police, for greater voice by the minorities with larger tax-exemption (so they may "enjoy the fruits of more government programs"). The "people" will be appealed to, as though the "people's voice" was not central among the principles upon which our constitutional form of local self-government was established by our Founding Fathers.

Several outstanding authorities have contributed their judgments in this book and have suggested some of the things that need doing—need doing by responsible, concerned citizens of all ages.

Central to it all, however, we reiterate three things:

FIRST: the Goal—the ends sought remain the same—*A Socialist America.*

SECOND: This can be achieved by either *politically peaceful* means OR *anarchistic destructive* and *violent* means.

THIRD: That BOTH means—*peaceful* and *violent*—can be expected to be employed persistently but in a more sophisticated manner than before.

We trust the background in these pages and the various suggestions for countering this stepped-up drive to Socialism will be useful to you.

SECTION I

GUERRILLA WARFARE IN THE UNITED STATES

EARLY IN 1970 J. Edgar Hoover said, "There exists in this country a strong Marxist revolutionary youth movement . . . A failure to recognize the seriousness of this threat could do great damage to the United States . . ."

On August 24, 1970, after viewing the wreckage of the Science Building, State Attorney General Robert Warren of Wisconsin said, "The bombings at the University of Wisconsin mark the beginning of an outright revolution . . ."

Yet, it appears that the President's Commission on Campus Unrest had been asking at Kent State University and elsewhere: Who fired the first shot . . . the law enforcement officers under attack—or a sniper? The inference was that, if it were the law enforcement officers, the snipers and militants were justified. The background and motivation of the militants and those who were coaching them seemed irrelevant.

They didn't seem to care about the graduate students who had been egging students on with the theme that the President was murdering the Constitution by invading Cambodia; how draft card burners were encouraged days before the violence happened; or that morals had been sinking for some time as evidenced by drinking at the downtown bars, use of drugs, co-ed pregnancies, and increasing use of obscenities. Although students engaged in such activities were indeed in the minority, where, one could ask, was the administration? What did it attempt to do to teach American principles, morals and decent behavior? Who were the outside agitators? The fire starters? The student brawlers? The citizens had long been concerned about the "new life style" that threatened their decent city. Did the Commission try to find out "why"? Does anyone suppose that when Bernardine Dohrn spoke on campus on April 28, 1969 that she was teaching "togetherness" or "love thy neighbor"?

And only two weeks before the violence Jerry Rubin, speaking on Kent campus, said, "Quit being students . . . become criminals . . . kill your parents . . ." no professor nor

Students at Kent State University (Ohio) chant and give "peace" sign to about 500 Ohio National Guardsmen and scores of other police early on May 4, 1970, as clashes between Kent State University students and police go into their third day. Five students have been injured, and more than fifty arrested, and the Army R.O.T.C. building was destroyed by fire.   UPI student challenged him! Not a word of it was reported nor repudiated by the campus newspaper. And the Students for a Democratic Society had been operating there for over two years. Their program appears to be clear advocacy of violence, but its importance is less than clear in the Commission report.

In its report, the Commission, while disapproving destruction by students, seemed in a subtle way to place the blame for the tragic deaths on the law enforcement agencies. There is much evidence that many of those killed or injured were actively engaged in taunting the Guard and being in the forefront of the mob of militants opposing the forces brought in to establish order. Nothing is said about *who* caused the violence, *who* taught students disregard for law and order, *who* stimulated the criminal attitudes of students, or *who* encouraged the destruction of property.

Since then the local Grand Jury has indicted 25 persons, including students, a professor, and others, among them some injured during the violence. Other students have presented the Kent State President a petition with over 2,000 names, blaming outside agitation for the tragedy.

DISASTROUS PERMISSIVENESS

At a news conference in Washington, D.C., on November 9, 1970, the President of Kent State, Robert I. White, took exception to the local Grand Jury report. Although he asserted that academic communities cannot be sanctuaries for lawbreakers, he added "neither is the academic community a place where ideas, *no matter how offensive*, are to be suppressed." (*emphasis added*)

On February 18, 1971, Mr. White announced his resignation to become effective September 15, 1971. He may have heard from the citizens or the serious students' parents!

Mr. White apparently hopes, however, to stay on as a professor - preferably in education.

While the majority of students and many faculty members apparently were opposed to the radical programs, several radical-socialist-revolutionary groups were organized and operating at least two years before the violence erupted in May

1970. This included the Students for a Democratic Society, the Young Socialist Alliance, the Weatherman, the Progressive Labor Party and the Revolutionary Youth Movement. Some have never had legal status on campus. In addition, outside agitators like Mark Rudd, Rennie Davis and Jerry Rubin appeared on campus and spoke.

Early in January 1971, a free mini-bus service was started by some businessmen for transporting students from campus to downtown taverns between 10 P.M. and 2:30 A.M. daily! It is reported that taverns are crowded with the "kids."

Could it be that these kinds of permissiveness explain why neither the president nor any professor or student challenged Jerry Rubin when he said to the students on this campus two weeks before the violence, "... *You must become criminals. You must kill your parents.*"

Have we arrived at the point in America where murder can be advocated in an institution where "searching for the truth" is its assumed central purpose?

Have we come to the point in our history where loyal young Americans in the State Guard are to place their lives on the line—unarmed against a mob led by anarchists and revolutionaries who have the implied support of members of investigating Commissions under the guise of dissent? And are the great majority of students, who are law abiding and seeking an education, to be terrorized by a militant minority and their proper education impaired or denied?

Are our laws so weak, our courts so inadequate, and the campus administrators so permissive that programs advocated for our destruction on the campuses must be allowed under the facade of free speech, or legitimate dissent?

Or, have our educational institutions become void of traditional moral training? Could it be that parents have abdicated their responsibility so completely that they care not *what* goes on in school? Have they failed in their job of moral training?

It is most likely that a small minority is casting the dark shadow over all students. How else can we reconcile the behavior of some youth with the assumed idealism of all young people?

The University of Wisconsin is another one of the many institutions that have a long history of liberal orientation. During the recent period of campus unrest, it has been among those accommodating many kinds of student demands. Yet, that did not satisfy the anarchists. Their science building was a casualty of militant action on August 24, 1970.

No wonder Bernard C. Ziegler, President of the University of Wisconsin Board of Regents, was disturbed over the findings of the President's Commission on Campus Unrest. "The report," he said on September 28, 1970, "should have pointed the finger of blame right at the students and faculties . . . the students should have been told: 'Look, the country is doing its share. You do yours'."

Instead it appears that the Commission wants the President of the United States to play God, and solve the problems that the Socialists in and out of government, in and out of colleges, in and out of the news media have been creating and planning for since at least the turn of the century.

On October 1, 1970, syndicated columnist James J. Kilpatrick, writing in *The Washington Evening Star*, said: "The President's Commission on Campus Unrest laid a neat trap for Nixon in its generally useless report last weekend. But the trap is a little too neat, a little too contrived, to have much political effect . . ." Then he continued:

". . . It was a colossal waste of money, and was bound to be. Such commissioners as Rhodes went on the trail in July with their prejudices neatly packed, and never bothered to open their bags.

"By spreading blame like mayonnaise, across the whole sandwich, the commission achieved one massive, equivocal waffle."

". . . In passing" writes Clare Boothe Luce in the *Honolulu* magazine, "there is irony and humor in the picture of the Intellectuals who demand White House leadership and 'national unity' but can 'lead' their own campus only by bending to student demands, and who violently disagree among themselves in the solution to the most crucial question that faces them: how to maintain order on their own campuses. . . ."

SOCIALIST AGITATORS
AND OTHER INTELLECTUALS OVERLOOKED

Overlooked completely by former Governor William W. Scranton's group was the penetrating part so-called campus intellectuals, Socialist teachers and other pseudo-intellectuals had in shaping the minds and morals of their students.

Rather prophetically, *The Wall Street Journal* summed it up in its July 27, 1970 editorial entitled "What Students Are Taught", as follows:

". . . To an important extent, surely, student disruption grows out of the intellectual currents of our time. In this and other ways we are only beginning to understand, these currents have grown extraordinarily perverse to the interests of society.

"A number of scholars have in various ways touched on this malaise among the intellectually oriented elite. To take only the academic luminaries, we think of Daniel P. Moynihan, Nathan Glazer, Edward C. Banfield, Zbigniew Brzezinski, Daniel Boorstin. We might also add Michael Lerner, for his article on 'elite bigotry' in *The American Scholar,* and Andrew M. Greeley for his recent witty and perceptive contribution to the *New York Times Magazine,* 'Intellectuals as an Ethnic Group.' It might pay Governor Scranton's group to ask such people whether student disruption might be related to the current mood of the adult intelligentsia.

"For our part, we are quite convinced that disruption by students has deep roots in the attitudes of professors. This is not merely a matter of an academic fringe actually advocating anarchy, though that plays a certain part. Nor is it merely a matter of the typical faculty lacking the courage and cohesion to discipline unruly students. For a faculty could hardly be expected to expel students for an excess of zeal in expressing the very attitudes the faculty is so proud to have instilled in them.

"Chief among these is the notion that the ills of the nation and the world would prove quite tractable if only everyone listened more to the intellectuals. The intellectual has always felt himself uniquely qualified to run society, but never before the 1960s had this feeling found such support: A growing social class oriented to the intellectual, almost complete penetration of the media, acceptance at court during the Kennedy era.

"As the intellectual class grew in prestige and influence, though, the content of its thought grew only in dog matism. The Vietnam war became not only mistaken but immoral; American society became irredeemably racist. The dogma carries a suspect tinge.

"Too many of the mistakes in Vietnam were made by representatives of the intellectual class that gave the State Department its undersecretaries, the White House its basement advisers and the Pentagon its civilian whiz-kids. Too often the denunciations of racists served mostly to make the denouncer feel virtuous. But no matter, the conclusions became part of the intellectual class-creed, and history may yet view the 1960s as the decade in which the prevailing liberal orthodoxy reduced itself to an absurdity.

"For many students, university experience during this decade amounted to a force-feeding in these doctrines: That intellectual prescriptions can solve all problems (even those that have resisted solution for a millenium), that the proper prescriptions are those favored by the intellectual class (no matter how narrow a social stratum it occupies), that failure to adopt these 'obvious' prescriptions must mean political leaders are stupid or venal (never that they are sensitive to a broader range of society or a broader range of reality).

"There are of course outstanding professors who apply their critical skills even to this creed, but they are few. The intellectual class is remarkably inbred; a sample survey of political scientists finds, for example, that only 12% of them voted for President Nixon. Given an intense and one-sided socialization in this narrow class, students not surprisingly develop a sturdy sense of self-righteousness, which is the stock-in trade for those who would occupy buildings, close campuses and bully professors who dissent from the dogma.

"The recent outbreak of disruption is not too surprising in light of the intellectual trends on campus, but it certainly is ironic. For the notions of intellectual preeminence that did so much to foster the disruptions have also proved their first casualty. How will serious men take an intellec-

tual class that is unable to govern a university, but pre-
sumes to govern the whole society?"

Dr. Miller Upton, President of Beloit College, puts the
finger on another related aspect of "where we are." "I have
just about reached the end of my tolerance for the way our
society seems to have sympathetic concern only for the mis-
fits, the pervert, the drug addict, the drifter, the ne'er-do-
well, the maladjusted, the chronic criminal, the under-
achiever, the loser . . . in general, the underdog." "It seems to
me". . . says Dr. Upton . . . "we have lost touch with reality
and become warped in our attachments, if not in
fact . . . psychotic."

And Dr. John A. Howard, President of Rockford (Illinois)
College, demonstrates that at least some college administrators know that our current crisis involves the destruction of our free enterprise system.

Speaking on the Manion Forum, August 2, 1970, he said:

". . . my basic concern is that a great portion of the
opinion makers in this country, particularly the intellectual community, doesn't understand how the private enterprise system operates, nor its incredible success, as contrasted with any other economic system. This is illustrated
by the recent campaign to make General Motors 'responsible.' which undertook to try to elect three directors to
the board of General Motors and to have the Articles of
Incorporation changed.

"The directors were to have been Betty Furness, a
clergyman from Washington, D.C. and a college professor.
Now, of course, everybody would like to have General
Motors and every other corporation responsible, but it's
this vicious kind of slogan which is doing so much damage.
Responsible compared to what? Responsible in what?

"This campaign talks about the public interest. Well, of
course, everybody would like to have corporations operate
in the public interest, but who is to define it? Is Betty
Furness? Are we sure that what she would believe to be
the public interest would be identical with what you and I
and everybody else would consider to be the public
interest?

"The campaign sent letters out to the presidents of all the colleges and universities in the country asking them to vote their GM stock in their endowment portfolios in behalf of their effort. At Rockford College we, of course, voted for management in that election. Our concern for their endowment interest is to have the securities which we hold produce the best revenue possible so that we can pay our salaries and carry on the work at the college. I think that people involved in the campaign either don't understand the private enterprise system or else it's an intentional effort to confuse the public and get control of the corporation. . . ."

CAMPAIGN OF BOMBINGS

While our attentions have been called to the wave of bombings in 1970, the media—press, radio, and television—have said very little about the fact that these bombings are *not* the work of isolated nuts or "crazies" or that the techniques employed are *not* learned by some mysterious osmotic process. Therefore, the public doesn't realize that these acts are part and parcel of orchestrated guerrilla warfare.

In one month alone, March 1970, at least 62 attacks on various institutions in several ways were conducted by left-wing guerrillas including the Weatherman. These institutions included industrial headquarters like International Business Machines, Mobil Oil, and General Telephone in New York. Time bombs were discovered in the Army installations in Portland, Oregon, Brooklyn, New York and Oakland, California. A post office was dynamited in Seattle, Washington, the Federal Building was firebombed in Champagne, Illinois, and a courthouse blown up in Cambridge, Maryland. Eight colleges felt the impact of various forms of physical destruction as well as six high schools.

A few figures should put the crises in better perspective, as reported by various government agencies for 1970 (up to December 1) as follows:

1. There were over 200 street riots and disturbances. Twenty five persons were killed.

2. Nearly 1,000 bombings were reported and the targets were businesses and government buildings as well as private homes. (From January 1969 to April 1970 there were 4,330 bombings, 1,475 attempted bombings, and 35,129 threats to bomb. Bombings were responsible for the deaths of 43 people and $21.8 million of property damage.)

3. During the 1969-1970 college year nearly 1,800 student demonstrations, sit-ins, arson, building seizures and other forms of violence were reported on campuses. Eight persons were killed, 462 injured and 7,500 were arrested.

4. During the same period, a total of 530 disturbances attributed to racial causes were reported in grade and high schools.

5. At least 88 policemen were killed.

6. Bombings and other forms of destruction caused a total loss of $1,471,875.00 to federal and non-federal property on campuses during the two school years from 1968 to 1970.

7. More than $102,650.00 was collected by over 50 radical speakers on campuses since February, 1969. While some sources of funds are not known, reports show that student as well as institutional funds were used. In some cases Students for a Democratic Society and the Student Mobilization Committee to End the War in Vietnam sponsored the speakers.*

8. More bombings and blackmail techniques can be expected.

Thus, while current bombings are indeed part of the revolution, and more are expected in 1971, this form of the revolution—guerrilla warfare—began at least as early as 1965—and for specific purposes.

But the planned revolution involves more than destruction by bombings—and dates back over a half century, as we will summarize in a section of this brief review.**

*See Appendix for details and recent dollar totals.

**The campaign to discredit J. Edgar Hoover and the F.B.I. by radicals, liberals and a few politicians, of course, gives aid and comfort to the anarchists and revolutionaries conducting guerrilla warfare.

SECTION II

ORGANIZED AGITATORS DOING SOCIALISTS' WORK

WRITING IN *The Honolulu Star Bulletin* early in the spring of 1970, Clare Boothe Luce, author and former U.S. Ambassador to Italy, makes several important points. After referring to many consequences of campus violence under the caption of "Organized Agitators," she says:

". . . Here one should mention a situation that deserves far more attention than it is getting—many of the activists who appear during campus demonstrations are not enrolled students. They are organized agitators, who have been sent into crowds of students to egg them on to violence, and these may well be Communists. During demonstrations they operate like Mao's guerrillas (swimming like fish), among the aroused students.

"But whether or not any, or all, of the on-campus or off-campus New Left activists are Communists, what is now clear is that they are doing communism's work. Who will dispute that the campus demonstrations of the past few weeks have been a disaster for the U.S. image abroad, and a tremendous victory for Moscow, Peking and Hanoi?

"Public opinion will, of course, assign some of the blame to the . . . permissiveness of parents. Some will fall on the heads of the editors and commentators, who have helped to make heroes of the New Activists, first, by attributing to them an idealism and love of peace that their own actions belie; second, by giving them excessive news coverage, and neglecting those students, the majority, who disapprove of them.

"(For example, the Honolulu papers gave the University of Hawaii students who seized the Reserve Officers Training Corps buildings the full-blown front page treatment. But Miss Vicki Webster, the gallant miss who defied and repulsed them, when they tried to take over the Women's Auxiliary ROTC building, did not rate a picture anywhere in the paper! Similarly, no names and no pictures were printed of the members of the Student Council who subsequently voted to keep ROTC on campus.)

ASSIGNING BLAME

"The press itself may be counted on, in assessing blame, to blame such vague concepts as the generation gap, the spirit of the times, or the mood of the country. Partisan editors will, of course, seek to blame the violence of the recent demonstrations on President Nixon's Cambodian decision, ignoring the fact that the phenomenon of campus violence was evident long before he entered the White House.

"But the reasonable rule in assigning blame is that blame falls where responsibility lies. This rule was observed by President Kennedy, when he took full responsibility for the Bay of Pigs, and again by President Nixon, when he took full responsibility for the Cambodian decision. It was also humorously noted by President Truman, who kept a sign on his White House desk that read, 'The buck stops here.'

"The person who must assume full responsibility for what happens on a campus is the man who has been given the authority over the campus—the university's president. University presidents who repeatedly try to shirk or evade their prime responsibility for maintaining order, and preserving the climate of academic freedom, should be promptly cashiered by the boards of regents, or the trustees. (That is their responsibility.)

"Perhaps some such rule as three violent demonstrations, and the president is out, would be useful. Presidents who sincerely feel that the task assigned to them, by virtue of their office, is too onerous, complex, or dangerous, can always take the honorable course, followed by Thomas, Hamilton, Kirk, Kerr and others—and resign.

"The individual student or faculty member, of course, is to be blamed, and punished, for his own individual acts, wherever these acts are illegal, or violent. And the individual faculty member must also be held accountable for his own illegal acts. (Reason is overthrown by the spectacle of Dr. Oliver Lee, an open enthusiast for Mao Tse-tung's Communist dictatorship, taking liberal President [Harlan] Cleveland [of the University of Hawaii] to task in court for a suspected lack of devotion to the First Amendment!)

Yippie leader Jerry Rubin, 33, free in $25,000 bail after his conviction as one of the Chicago Seven in February 1970, chats with friends while attending a rally at Madison Square Garden, N.Y., March 12, advocating peace in Vietnam and a reordering of the nation's priorities. Earlier in the day he told a rally at City College that he was proud of the accusations that the defendants' conduct at the Chicago conspiracy trial had destroyed the court system. UPI

WHAT TO DO

"Henceforth, college authorities must make it plain that any faculty member who counsels a student to perform an illegal act, or who participates in that act, will be fired. They must also make it plain to the student body that any student who engages in any illegal act, or act of violence, or who presents a 'non-negotiable demand' will henceforth be presented with a non-negotiable expulsion. And, if expulsion shall then be followed by violent student demonstrations, that [they] will immediately close down the university, until reason reasserts itself.

"Presidents who follow this course will (one hopes) have the wholehearted support of the community and of the overwhelming majority of parents. For it is impossible to believe that parents will be willing much longer to pay out three to four-thousand hard-earned dollars a year to have the idealism and youthful impatience of their sons and daughters exploited by anarchists, nihilists, and Communists, especially when this exploitation can lead their children into the police courts—and may lead them to their death."

SECTION III

DESTRUCTION TAUGHT ON CAMPUS

IN THE BOOK *Teachers of Destruction—Their Plans for a Socialist Revolution*, published by the Citizens Evaluation Institute, the author reports evidence for answers to important questions that the violence and bombings have raised. For instance, WHO is behind this destructive revolution? WHO has set student criminal attitudes in motion? WHO is doing the basic planning? WHERE is it done? WHAT are the real objectives? HOW LONG has the process of destroying the American System been going on? WHERE is the money coming from to finance our destruction? This eyewitness account of the Socialist Scholars' meetings for the past six years is an unequivocal documented report.

The author shows that the revolution we are witnessing has deep roots. She demonstrates that the underlying causes for which so-called dissent is given justification have been cultivated for a long time. (Many of these problems stem from the multitude of welfare state projects developed over the last 30 years and not from the free-choice, free-enterprise system, which is now greatly restricted and in the process of being demolished.)

Her study shows that much of the basic planning for destruction involves dedicated Socialist school administrators and teachers. They really do not seek to correct faults on the campus. Rather, the goal they seek is a complete Socialist revolution by violent or peaceful means—or both.

Violence is just one tactic in our destruction. As a symbol, abolishment of private property and free enterprise has meaning to the destroyers. Their other tactics should also be clear signals to all patriotic citizens. For as J. Edgar Hoover says:

"...The whole history of Judaic-Christian culture is ridiculed, mocked, and scorned. Out of this rejection of a belief in democratic values, grow dangerous processes..."

MORALITY OUT — NEW LIFE STYLE IN

These processes are signals foreboding other revolutionary techniques and crucial consequences. They glorify obscenity, drug culture, sex perversion, kidnapping, blackmail, bombing, arson, and murder. They espouse spending ourselves into bankruptcy, and disarming our local and national defenses and security forces.

Many college presidents, government officials, and clergymen dismiss student violence as a passing phenomenon, with the soothing cliché that "America is so strong she cannot be destroyed." Others assert that the goals sought (Socialism) are desirable, and should be achieved by peaceful means.

And while the liberal "intellectuals" promote communal cohabitation, affluent teenagers begging on the streets, pagan pornography and wanton sex—justifying it all as "youth searching for a new life style" or a "new Culture" (which includes the prevalence of venereal disease now beyond epidemic proportions and uncontrollable shoplifting amounting to $3 billion in 1970)—the Presidential Commission on Pornography calls for the repeal of current restraints on filth with the excuse that it's all harmless! The Commission was headed by William B. Lockhart, Dean, Law School of the liberal University of Minnesota.

Even the Supreme Court has made it easier for the purveyors of filth. And the American Civil Liberties Union, the National Education Association and the Association of American Publishers announced that they joined hands, seemingly to find something good in pornography and not make it more difficult to produce and distribute it.

Some tax-supported agencies are trying to inventory what is wrong with our system to justify student violence as a cover-up with the excuse of "dissent." Such inventories seem to serve as another basis for calling for more socialistic schemes. The message seems clear—spend more taxpayers' money—give back some with no strings attached and camouflaged as free—move toward more and more government intervention in the free market and local self-government until all our Judaic-Christian moral values and the "establishment" are destroyed.

Some universities, including tax-supported ones, are trying to promote the "new life style" in the name of education in unique ways.

As an example, the freshmen orientation program for incoming students at the University of Washington openly states:

"Tuesday, 4 p.m. SOCIAL AND SEXUAL RELATIONSHIPS: - This discussion or 'rap' session may cover everything from dating to sleeping with someone, men's and women's roles in our society, any aspect of interpersonal relationships, contraceptives, ways to meet people, or anything else that might be on your mind. . . .

"Tuesday, 8:30 p.m. CELEBRATING BEING ALIVE: - What we do is to bring in a very good stereo system, some fantastic tapes, a strobe light, incense,

Gas-masked policeman throws a tear gas canister into a crowd on April 29, 1970 after violence erupted on the Ohio State University (Columbus) campus. Over twenty five persons, including police, were injured. Six were shot. Nearly one hundred people were arrested. UPI

punch, soft things to sit on, etc., and take it all into our
dining room and block all the light from outside - what
we really do is provide a space in which people can do
what they want to do and feel good. When you feel glad
and you're alive and manifest that in some action, you
are celebrating."

How is your school, your university, your college doing it?

To understand better the source and meaning of what is
happening we must realize three hard facts: *the basic planning for a socialist revolution is not new; the infinite variety
of methods planned for and being used to achieve the socialist goals are both violent and peaceful; and the innocent and
loyal Americans are being duped into aiding and abetting the
disciplined anarchists in their designs for our destruction.*

SECTION IV

YOUNG PEOPLE BECOME MARXIST DUPES

". . . The tolerance that many students showed to SDS,"
says Clare Boothe Luce in the *Honolulu* magazine, "was
because its members were always ready and well-prepared
with arguments which lifted any possible burden of guilt
from student shoulders and transferred it to the White
House, the Pentagon and the State Department. Large
sections of the media and many politicians (often for reasons of political prejudice and self-interest) encouraged the
students in their feelings of righteous indignation against
the government. . . ."

ALLAN C. BROWNFELD, a member of the staff, Senate
Subcommittee on Internal Security, has made a special study
of the revolutionary voices and forces at work to capture the
minds and morals of high school students. Writing in the
November 1970 issue of *Christian Economics,* he says:

"... A national Students for a Democratic Society high school policy was promulgated in late 1968 at an S.D.S. National Council meeting in Boulder, Colorado, where a special 'high school resolution' was passed.

"The resolution called for (1) the hiring of a national high school co-ordinator, (2) regional organizations and local chapters of S.D.S. to make high school organization a large part of their program, and (3) the national circulation of an underground paper currently being published by the Los Angeles High School chapter of S.D.S.

"An S.D.S. 'Organizers' Manual for the Spring offensive in 1969 contains the following information:

'It has become clear within the last year or so that high school organizing—particularly working class high schools—is of vital importance to the development of our movement. High Schools are almost uniformly like prisons; they teach nothing but the crudest versions of bourgeois ideology, impose offensive disciplinary rules, spending most of their energy keeping kids off the streets while waiting to enter the job market or the army. Further, high school students are rebelling with greater and greater frequency, and make the possibility of cross-city and working class youth movements much more possible.'

"In July of 1969 a delegation of S.D.S. leaders was part of a larger delegation of Americans who went to Cuba to meet with Viet Cong and North American representatives. In a special 'Vietnam Supplement' to *New Left Notes* published after that visit, Vietnamese advice on the best type of recruit for the New Left was quoted: 'At the meeting in Cuba with PRG (Provisional Revolutionary Government of South Vietnam, basically consisting of elements of the Viet Cong), Van Ba (head of the PRG delegation) told us: "When you go into the city, look for the person who fights hardest against the cops. That's the one you talk all night with. Don't look for the one who says the best thing. Look for the one who fights."

"*The New York Post's* Leonard Lyons recently carried this item: A Radcliffe student who has friends in S.D.S.'s Weatherman faction spoke to some who had just returned from helping harvest Castro's sugar crop. They told her that one of the plans they had discussed was to kill the entire population of a village in America. This, they felt, would dramatize for Americans the massacre at My Lai.

"In hearings held in the House of Representatives during October, 1969, testimony brought out the fact that the S.D.S. was following a planned program to build a fighting cadre among high school youths and established three communes in Columbus, Ohio, during the summer of 1969.

FREE BEER AND GUNS

"S.D.S. pursued a program of attempting to talk to and recruit high school students engaged in summer sessions and to incite and inflame teenagers on the street. The S.D.S. activities in the high schools, essentially consisting of passing out literature and talking with students, were conducted before classes in the morning, during lunch breaks and after classes in the afternoon. On July 15, 1969, obscenities were painted on the walls of five Columbus high schools.

"Two teenagers from Columbus confirmed that S.D.S. activists had advocated theft, arson and bombings, as well as the killing of policemen. The S.D.S. members had initiated such discussions with youths of high school age in July 1969, at a school recreation area popular with teenagers. Lured by an offer of free beer and a gun display, the youngsters even brought along their friends for a second meeting and another dose of S.D.S. propaganda. The teenagers were told that if they would organize with S.D.S., the organization would provide them with guns and teach them to 'kill pigs' (police officers) . . .

MEETING THE CHALLENGE . . . THERE IS HOPE

"One possible method of meeting this challenge has been provided by the public school system of New York City. High school students returning to class there receive in-depth training in an old word—RESPONSIBILITY.

"A new policy statement outlining a behavior code adopted by the Board of Education pinpoints rights and responsibilities of senior high school students in various areas where there has been confusion and sometimes sharp controversy.

" 'A major goal of the document,' says Irving Anker, acting superintendent, 'is to establish a new trust, one based on the humane values of self-respect and respect for others. *No student has the right to interfere with the education of his fellow students.* If dialogue is interrupted or destroyed, then the bonds that hold us together are broken. It is thus the responsibility of each student to respect the rights of all who are involved in the educational process.'

"The plan provides for a parent-student-faculty consultative council that will meet monthly to discuss any matter relating to one or more of the city's 91 academic and vocational high schools. It also establishes a sub-committee to consider matters of schoolwide concern submitted by individual students.

"New rules regarding pupil suspension supersede previous measures.

'The school principal shall have emergency power to suspend a student from participation in regular school activity when he determines that the overt behavior of that student prevents the orderly operation of the class or other activities or presents a clear and present danger of physical injury to school personnel or students. . . .' "

SINCERE STUDENTS WILL ACT

In the December 5, 1970 issue of *Human Events,* Walter W. Seifert, associate professor in the School of Journalism, Ohio State University, and member of the Board of Scholars, Citizens Evaluation Institute, recounts a great story of how sincere students can be mobilized to help save their educational institutions.

He describes some of the problems that a small informal group of students faced and overcame in mobilizing student support for what colleges are supposed to do — educate.

He goes on to relate several significant consequences as follows:

Fist fight erupts in front of Boston's English High October 1, 1969, when members of SDS tried to prevent students from entering the school. The SDS members planted themselves on top of the steps in front of the building chanting about black and brown power. The fighting was short-lived when SDS retreated. One instructor was injured.   UPI

Editor's note: "The ability to manipulate people through violence and mass media has never been greater," Dave Gilbert, SDS, said on a previous occasion.

". . . Coppeler and Blackshaw [two students] meanwhile made national news. They organized 'Students for Majority Rights' and filed a $1-million lawsuit 'to hold faculty and student disrupters liable for the consequences of their actions.' Their petition for a court injunction against nine student leaders of the Strike Coalition was granted. (As this is written, the damage suit is still on the docket, and a target faculty member is now teaching at a school in New Hampshire that has less than 400 students.)

"Both groups found the local, state and national media quite responsive to their cause. Wire services carried stories that hit front pages across the nation, including the *New York Times, Washington Post, Chicago Tribune* and *Los Angeles Times. Parade* magazine carried a full page.

"Editors and commentators seemed eager to balance the tide of negative campus news with this more positive move. Many readers sent money in, and some expressed amazement that any moderate students would stand. Coppeler's page ad in the *Alumni Monthly* proved specially productive. A network TV show paid off. So did ads in the Columbus papers.

"Midway in May, when Ohio State reopened, it was obvious most students did not favor the strike. 'They voted with their feet by attending classes,' Forster [a public relations student] said. Less than 10 per cent went to the noonday strike rallies, and this dwindled day by day. The violence ceased entirely. In June the university held commencement on schedule. . ."

Professor Seifert adds:

". . . It would be wrong to give these students complete credit for the calm, rational atmosphere on our campus thus far this fall. Many others helped, including our state legislature, courts and administrators. . ."

There has been constructive action by those representing the majority of sincere students on other campuses. Two examples from the January issue of *Reader's Digest* further illustrate the point made by Professor Seifert. At the University of Florida, a law student campaigned for president of the student government on a platform advocating more campus police. In a field of five candidates, he won 53 percent of the votes. A student at San Fernando Valley State College mounted an "Open Campus Movement" to fight radical violence.

Young Americans For Freedom, for instance, have been working on constructive projects for a long time.

These examples also give hope. There are, of course, many others which go unreported.

GRADE SCHOOL CHILDREN'S MINDS POLLUTED

The training for contempt for decency and law and order has penetrated even below high school age through grade school channels. A book, published by Simon and Schuster of New York, entitled *Sylvester and the Magic Pebble,* is a case in point.

It is illustrated, showing pigs in law officers' uniforms. Deputy Sheriff Donald Belcher, of Prince Georges County, Maryland, discovered it when his nine-year-old daughter brought the book home from the school library. *The Washington Evening Star,* November 10, 1970, related Mr. Belcher's reaction as follows:

". . . It's not funny. We're trying to do our job as police officers and then our own kids bring things like this home. The kids have heard so much about this pig thing and the police . . . that they are believing policemen are all pigs and animals," he said.

". . . She was reading it last night when she giggled and pointed to the full color picture of the police station and said, 'Look at the pigs, daddy.'

"I blew my stack," Belcher said, describing his emotions when he saw the police station scene of pig policemen talking to Sylvester's [the character in the plot] parents. "She didn't know the meaning of 'pigs' until the riots and all on television, but she now identifies pigs with police officers and the point got across with the picture," Belcher said.

It is clear that parents and leaders must look into the whole schoolbook problem from kindergarten through college and ask, "How did these books get here?" "Who selected them?" "Why?" "Who pays to pollute the minds of young people—whether it is in politics, morals or economics?"

Is a starting point a complete and critical examination of the so-called Social Science Studies program and all the textbooks associated with it in your schools?

SECTION V

SOCIALIST REVOLUTION LONG PLANNED

PLANNING FOR A Socialist takeover really began in America at least as early as 1905.

It may be useful to readers that we recount some of this little known background. In so doing the reader will find names that are active in recent political and academic activities as well as in the arts and news media.

One of the anarchist organizations formed at the turn of the century was the International Workers of the World, known for years by its critics as the I Won't Workers (IWW). Although it appeared to fade out, it has recently been rejuvenated on the campus at Berkeley, California.

The formal planning for the organization, however, that has had a key influence in the drive to socialism in the U.S.A. began with a meeting of about 100 men and women in a room over Peck's Restaurant in New York City on September 12, 1905. Their announced purpose was *"to promote an intelligent interest in socialism among undergraduate and graduate students and professors."*

Among those who called this organization meeting were: Clarence S. Darrow, Jack London, Upton Sinclair, and Walter Lippmann.

The Intercollegiate Socialist Society resulted, which immediately proceeded to establish campus chapters. Norman Thomas and Harry Laidler became co-directors. Ironically, in retrospect, the first chapter was established at Columbia University, where much of the planning and action for today's revolution has taken place.

Soon a chapter was formed at Yale, where Dr. Kingman Brewster is now President. His record for Socialist ideas and yielding to student demands needs no elaboration. Benjamin Spock, M.D., a Yale graduate, is well known for his activities with the New and Old Left. He is only one of countless others of prominence who have been involved in promoting current militancy and violence.

The next I.S.S. chapter was set up at Harvard in 1906. To show a certain amount of academic independence, this group called itself the Harvard Socialist Club. Future columnist Walter Lippmann was its President. Among present day Socialist professors and exponents with Harvard ties are Arthur M. Schlesinger, Jr., and Staughton C. Lynd, as well as the liberal Kennedy family. John Maynard Keynes, the designer of "new economics," also carried the Socialist banner there.

As the organization grew under the tutelage of the parent group in England, "The Fabians," such British Fabian Socialists as George Bernard Shaw, Ramsay MacDonald, Beatrice and Sidney Webb (who were financed by Joseph Fels of Fels-Naphtha Soap fame), and other well-known Socialists emerged. Among them were Eugene V. Debs and Paul Douglas. Later Douglas became a United States Senator and served three terms.

TACTICS CHANGE

When the leadership of the Intercollegiate Socialist Society discovered that Americans would not accept proposals clearly labeled "Socialism," their tactics changed in 1921. Semantics were introduced. A new facade—a "moral society" (meaning humanism) was to be created and the "two platoon" system became a useful technique.

The first step was to change the name. The ISS became the League for Industrial Democracy, under which name it still operates. They hoped this name would appeal to labor, to politicians, and to so-called liberals in general.

Their slogan proclaimed their goal—*"Education for a new social order based on production for use and not for profit."* And if you haven't read Marx, what's wrong with that? Some of their members in turn have been involved in forming Americans for Democratic Action, the American Civil Liberties Union, Students for a Democratic Society, the Center for Democratic Studies, the Council on Foreign Relations, and a host of other "fronts."

The employment of Socialist professors in the classrooms and administrative positions grew year by year. John Dewey, the permissive educator at Columbia; Arthur Holcomb, professor of Government at Harvard; Julius Bixler, President of Colby College; Alexander Meiklejohn, President of Amherst; Harold Taylor, President of Sarah Lawrence College; Robert Hutchins, former President, University of Chicago (now at the Center for the Study of Democratic Institutions); and many more.

Soon Socialist politicians came to the forefront, such as Senators Paul Douglas, Wayne Morse, Hubert Humphrey (later Vice President of the United States, and a professor at Macalester College, St. Paul, Minnesota, and elected again to the Senate in 1970), and Herbert Lehman.

The roster of those prominent in the literary world also grew to include Jack London, Upton Sinclair, Lincoln Steffens, Edna St. Vincent Millay and Louis Fischer.

Members of the clergy soon affiliated. Among them were Reinhold Niebuhr of Union Theological Seminary, John C. Bennett and Bishop James Pike.

Early in the 20's the League decided that it would be easier to infiltrate government than to destroy it by revolution, as the Marxists' goal proclaimed. Hence the tactic was to work from within departments and agencies and enlarge their economic and social functions. A few examples of what happened to some advocates of Socialistic schemes are:

Leland Olds became Chairman of the Federal Power Commission, Paul Porter became a professional diplomat, Oscar L. Chapman became Secretary of the Interior, Gordon Clapp served as head of the Tennessee Valley Authority, Ralph Bunche (assistant to Alger Hiss) joined the State Department and later the United Nations, Rexford G. Tugwell became Under-Secretary of Agriculture in the Roosevelt Administration. (All were ardent LID associates and supporters.) Their disciplines, writings or voices reached into nearly every phase of American Life.

Washington, D.C.: Jerry Rubin wearing a Santa Claus costume and pointing a toy water gun was barred from a hearing of the House Committee on Un-American Activities on December 4, 1970. The committee was investigating disorders surrounding the Democratic Convention at Chicago. Rubin, founder of the Yippies, said he was dressed as Santa Claus to ridicule the Committee by pointing up "the red peril" and choosing a costume with a seasonal motif. UPI

In a like manner, a host of organizations and fronts for Socialism and Marxism today stem directly or indirectly from the League for Industrial Democracy, although other influences were also involved.

Many other Socialist-oriented individuals cooperated with the League, some deceased, others active today. To list a few: Bayard Rustin (member, Board of Trustees, Notre Dame University), Stuart Chase, Walter Reuther, Trygve Lie, Eleanor Roosevelt, Harry Overstreet, Elmer Davis, Stephen Rauschenbusch, Professor Alvin Hansen, George Meany, Max Lerner, James B. Carey, Daniel T. Moynihan—and many more.

When, in 1964, an offshoot of the American Civil Liberties Union was formed—The National Committee to Abolish the House Un-American Activities Committee—more than 150 professors, deans and other educators were listed as sponsors. Also over 60 from the field of religion, 60 from arts and letters, nearly 75 from business, labor and the professions, and over 80 from "community" organizations were included.

It does not take much imagination to understand the extent of the influence on current disorders or the support they can give to those seeking to undermine our national security by those philosophically oriented to this National Committee's goals.

HOW A VETERAN SOCIALIST WORKS

Professors Rex Tugwell and Robert Hutchins represent the kind of Fabian Socialists who are today in key positions and are openly influencing the unsophisticated and calling for non-violent change, with their goals remaining the same— a Socialist America.

Dr. Tugwell served as professor of the "new" economics at several universities, including Columbia. He campaigned for Norman Thomas, when Communists openly supported him. He is credited as being the architect of the New Deal. He wrote a world constitution, released in 1948, designed to abolish all nations—(everyone to be ruled and managed by a single top-down government). He is now at the Center for the Study of Democratic Institutions in Santa Barbara, California, heading a team of "intellectuals."

The Center's latest product, recently announced in the press, is a radical, completely new constitution for the United States to replace our present one. It provides for a form of Socialism in the economic and political areas. If any part of it is adopted, it will move us further toward complete socialism by "peaceful means." The Center says it is designed to make our government "function better at a time of revolutionary change." It's what some liberals will be calling "socialism within our present system."

When columnist James J. Kilpatrick wrote that—"Rex Tugwell and Robert Hutchins emphasize that their draft [Constitution] is not for real—it is only for discussion . . .", Frank K. Kelly, Vice President of the Center, replied in the January 10, 1971 issue of *The Washington Star* ". . . Mr. Kilpatrick is naturally opposed to a constitution that recognizes the necessity of vesting basic powers in the national government. . . At the Center, we believe that discussion is a real and vital element in a free society and we want every citizen to have an opportunity to take part in it. . ." Translated this means that a big one-sided campaign to get the new constitution adopted is in the making.

And Dr. Hutchins, identified with scores of left wing associations of considerable influence, has since 1946 been a member of the Board of Editors of the *Encyclopaedia Britannica*. He is a Yale alumnus and also studied at Oberlin College. . . in the schools that have harbored Socialist teachers for a long time.

THE GOAL IS CONSTANT

The Socialist goal today is, as always,—a "classless" society whose controlled production is based on need and not on profit, and in which production is governed and distributed by the ruling elite. (The classless society phase is now in the process of being examined by a judge for implementation *by force in some school districts under court order* under the guise of integration!) Whether Socialism is achieved peacefully or by violence is not the issue. Both are being used.

SECTION VI

A SOURCE OF FOREIGN IDEOLOGY

ANTHONY HARRIGAN, EXECUTIVE Vice President of the Southern States Industrial Council, highlights another source of some of the ideology involved in our revolutionary destructive process.

In his analysis, he says:

". . . Significant change took place in the thirties and forties. A generation was involved in a world war in which ideology was a factor. At the same time, the United States gave refuge to many educated Europeans who were steeped in the absolutist doctrines of the continent. Many of these refugees became formidable figures in America's intellectual life. They stamped their ideological approach to public issues on a rising generation of writers, jurists and public officials. For the first time in American history, newcomers shaped the nation's thinking, instead of American society giving shape to the newcomers' vision of life in this land.

A NEW ACTIVIST MENTALITY

"America was not ready to receive such a transfusion of absolutist conceptions. American society had not evolved so as to be able to deal effectively with the sophisticated absolutism of European origin. The traditional pattern of life here had allowed different areas to live in different ways. Americans did not anticipate the conditioning of minds or centralization of opinion. Local loyalties and traditions were respected. The notion of the law as an instrument for accomplishing social revolution was alien to our people.

"Law, in the American sense, was designed to protect the individual from oppression and wrongdoing. It was regarded as a restraining influence, not as a monolithic, directing force. Such a non-absolutist attitude towards law, government and society was bitterly opposed by the Europeans who assumed commanding positions in the universities and the intellectual community off-campus.

*The traditional easy-going American approach to
national problems gave way to an angry, harsh, all-
out approach which stressed 'necessity.'*

"One of the first departments of American life to feel
the impact of the new intellectual approach was the law.
Activist judges swept aside the precedents born of generations of adjudicating disputes among American citizens,
states and the federal government. A passion for 'justice,'
narrowly defined and shaped to serve a particular
conception of government, became so strong in the fifties
and sixties that fundamental needs of society—under the
heading of law and order—were ignored or scorned.

FRUIT OF ACTIVISM: CONFLICT

"What happened in this period is that the conscience of
a large part of the nation was radicalized. In this process,
the electronic media, chiefly television, played a central
role. Television, as in the 'news' programs of the late
Edward R. Murrow, became an instrument of absolutists
who were trying to impose their conceptions on the American public. The cameras presented lawful authorities as
overbearing and brutal, but carefully avoided showing any
of the provocative acts engaged in by political activists.
Spokesmen for revolutionary change were given ample
time to make a powerful impact on national audiences.
Revolutionaries were presented as calm and logical. No
embarrassing questions were put to demonstration organizers. Their smooth words were recorded but not their
brutal or insulting actions. As a result, revolutionaries received a sympathetic feedback. Many young viewers were
fired with enthusiasm for turning America upside down.

CHALLENGE OF NAKED POWER

"The challenge to government and society is one of
naked power—the same challenge that the Nazis held up to
the German people in the 1930's. Concerned citizens often
ponder the ugly record of recent years: Watts, Detroit,
Newark, the yippie war against Chicago, the Easter bomb
plot in New York City, the junkets to Hanoi by various
American friends of Ho Chi Minh, the march on the Pentagon, the SDS coups at Columbia and Harvard and the

invasion of the Wisconsin Assembly. Nothing succeeds like success. Thus the abuse and terror continue: more threats of arson, militants shouting obscenities at churchmen gathered in convention, insults to judges on the bench and Black Panthers teaching children to kill policemen

THE FOLLY OF POWER WORSHIP

"The absolutists in our midst, who have caused this mess, started out justifying anything in the name of 'justice.' Now, they worship the absolute of power. They talk of 'participatory democracy,' but aim at an absolutist 'democracy' of their own making. Young men are told—and many are persuaded—that rioting and a touch of arson can bring a world without war, prejudice or hunger. Anyone who can believe that can believe anything.

"Ten or even five years ago, if America's leaders had appreciated the danger posed by absolutist conceptions, it would have been relatively easy to prepare universities for the coming assault, to stiffen the backbone and moral understanding of the churches and to prevent infiltration of the armed forces by militants. Because nothing was done to defuse the New Left and to pulverize its incipient absolutism, an evil has spread across the nation.

A DAZED CITIZENRY ASKS QUESTIONS

"The prestige and authority of the United States government has accumulated in the course of almost 200 years. Yet as our country approaches its bicentennial celebration, much already has been accomplished by the New Left to eradicate the esteem with which Americans have viewed their republic. Many citizens seem dazed by the efforts of those who distort and downgrade America. The U.S. public may be approaching the point where it doesn't know what to believe about the country. After years of ceaseless propaganda from homegrown haters of the United States, many Americans ask: Are our military leaders the cause of wars in the world today? Is the United States attacking a legitimate nationalist movement in Vietnam? Has our society adopted inhuman values?

On 5/19/70 Angela Davis told newsmen in Los Angeles that she may go to court to challenge the right of the University of California Regents to hire or fire her from her teaching job at UCLA. The Regents voted to decide the issue of her employment themselves and relieved school authorities from making any decision in the case of the admitted Communist professor. With Miss Davis is Professor Arnold Kaufman of the UCLA American Federation of Teachers, AFL-CIO, who said the AFT members would stand behind her in her fight to stay employed at the University. She is now (Mar. 3, 1971) awaiting trial in California on charges that she bought guns that were used in a court kidnapping case in which a judge was fatally shot. A battery of lawyers are arranging the defense, and a panel of 12 law professors are mounting a campaign of "social justice." Some teachers unions are putting up posters in school rooms. Who is financing this entire project in behalf of the self-confessed Communist professor is not clear.   UPI

"It's no wonder that such moral and intellectual confusion abounds. Never before in the nation's history has there been a studied attempt to change American psychology, to dissolve faith in America's achievements and values, to make dirty things of national symbols, to brain-wash the entire population and to create inside the country a parallel society of protesters who dissent from every action and value of the United States. We are witnesses, in other words, to an effort to transform our society by lies and violence and to liquidate its strength.

WHAT TO DO

"Survival requires that the federal and state governments use all their lawful authority to deter and isolate those who make a new religion or cult of violence against America and its institutions. Fortunately, the hard core of violence-oriented defectors from our society is still a small element in a nation of more than 200 million people.

PRESCRIPTION FOR PEACE WITH FREEDOM

"Stamping out the revolutionary movement will require unusual firmness and steadfastness. Americans place a high value on tolerance, and are reluctant to take vigorous measures against even the most open and notorious advocates of disorder. One is reminded of Hegel's dictum: 'History is not the realm of happiness.' This absolutist, whose conceptions have brought so much woe to mankind, was right in indicating that the carrying out of essential tasks of life and leadership can be an unhappy experience. We all yearn for the older America that was free of internal clashes and ideological strife. Nevertheless, we won't again enjoy the blessings of peace with freedom without administering unpleasant remedies, precisely as the physician often has to prescribe bitter medicine in order to restore health to a sick man.

"It is important to bear in mind that no irreversible law of breakdown rules our society. Breakdown occurs only where our society has failed to take preventive measures against the sick, aberrant element within. This destructive element, which is trying to destroy our way of life, has seceded from allegiance to America. An inner secession from our country is no more permissible in the late 20th Century, however, than a sectional secession was tolerable to the nation in the mid-19th Century.

WEAPONRY TO COMBAT INTERNAL BARBARIANS

"If the law is our shield and spear, it will have to be used in innovative fashion. Laws already on the books *can* be used in new ways.

"The law doesn't afford society sufficient protection where it only imposes punishment on those who commit acts of violence. To be adequate to the need of peace and justice for the community, the law has to apply against those who advocate violence and preach overthrow of the United States or its political subdivisions. Long ago, the American judiciary established the principle that freedom of speech does not extend to those who shout 'fire' in a crowded theater. Today, the entire United States is a crowded theater—a setting where an irresponsible act could result in a massive conflagration.

"If we accept the concept of law barring advocacy of revolution in any form or whatever guise, this understanding will crystallize out in the form of new rules for the operation of our society—rules that will make possible the security of America in the remaining years of this century.

THE DARKNESS CAN BE DISSIPATED

"The basic assumption we must make is that our society has a right to defend itself against those who would liquidate its values—that there is a superior wisdom in the organization and purposes of the United States that rightfully commands protection. To put this truth in other terms, America has an inalienable right to keep the internal barbarians at bay. The darkness that's fallen over America will lift if the American government and people offer total resistance to revolution."

MORE HOPE

One of the hopes appearing, however, is that some who have experienced the loss of freedom in Europe and Asia, are arising again as they have before to help lead the way to strengthen America's institutions based on liberty, law, order and justice.

The work of Benjamin Grob of Grafton, Wisconsin illustrates the point. He knows that true liberty (*not license*) is impossible in a society whose moral order has been destroyed.

ANTI—FILTH CAMPAIGN PAYS OFF

Mr. Grob came to America from Switzerland over 60 years ago. Taking advantage of the opportunities free America provided, Mr. Grob rose as one of America's finest precision tool manufacturers.

Two years ago, he discovered that the editor of several local papers in which he advertised was also printing an underground newspaper. Some issues contained material which ranked among the vilest pornography to be found anywhere, available to children and adults.

He decided not to support a printer of material of such low character and withdrew his advertising. He advised other advertisers of his actions and suggested they consider doing the same.

The printer was awarded the 1970 Elijah Parish Lovejoy award for "courage in journalism" by the Department of Journalism at Southern Illinois University.

Much of the liberal newspaper industry came to the printer's defense, including the *Milwaukee Journal.* Thereupon Mr. Grob offered the *Journal* $100,000.00 if they would print what he considered filthy and objectionable material appearing in the underground paper.

Lamely, the *Journal* replied that they couldn't do so because theirs was a "family newspaper."

The American Civil Liberties Union also came to the printer's defense.

But Mr. Grob held fast to his position. He was supported by many businessmen including the Wisconsin State Chamber of Commerce and citizens everywhere.

Result: 90% of the advertisers in the three weekly papers published by the printer withdrew their ads!

The printer was forced to sell two of his weekly papers. But he continued to print the underground sheet. His excuse was that the publishers of the underground paper had the right to dissent about the Vietnam War even though the paper used four letter words. And he said it was all legal.

The printer died on February 9, 1971. Whether another printer will help the pornographers publish the underground paper will undoubtedly be watched by decent local citizens. But Mr. Grob has already demonstrated what can be done.

If others will stand up and choose between decency and filth, as does Mr. Grob and his supporters, we may make a dent in the process of polluting the minds in other areas, instead of worrying about polluting "the physical environment" and hampering legitimate progress in the process.

LEFT-ORIENTED FACULTY MEMBERS

The kind of philosophical influence faculty members exert on students has been observed by many.

One of the most convincing yardsticks for estimating such influence is the evidence faculty members themselves have recently provided about their own bias.

In the fall of 1969, the Carnegie Commission on Higher Education conducted an opinion poll among 60,477 faculty members.

They were asked, for instance, to rate themselves on a five point scale ranging from "Conservative" through "Liberal." The results of this poll showed a range between 0.1% Conservative (Sociologists) the lowest, to 12.7% Conservative (Economists), the highest.

With such preponderance of left-oriented bias in the faculties, is it any wonder why college students are not getting the truth or developing a reasonable understanding of WHY and

WHAT makes our systems work and HOW it can properly be improved?

LIBERAL INDOCTRINATION RESULT

On February 16, 1971, the Gallup Poll reported the result of a similar self-classification survey with students. They were asked to rate themselves on a 5-point scale ranging from Far Left to Far Right.

One significant result was: 28 percent of the freshmen labeled themselves as Far Left or Left while 59 percent of the graduate students classified themselves in that category.

The lesson? It is clear that the longer the student is exposed to college professors the more liberal they become. The professor's self-rated bias does take effect.

WHAT TO DO

The challenge to reconstitute the faculties is clear. But achieving it is difficult. It will require massive effort by all who provide financial support to the institutions and those who seek to benefit by attending them.

How about your school's faculty?

What materials are in your school that teaches the truth about our system, of the free market, and local self-government? What are the materials used to teach high moral principles?

Should the whole system of tenure be critically examined in your schools and colleges? Why retain it and force a school to keep the incompetent and the radicals on the same basis as the proficient professor?

Some colleges have abandoned tenure with rewarding results. Pepperdine College of Los Angeles, California, for example, has pioneered in this and other areas of positive action.

WALL STREET JOURNAL

"We've discontinued the practice of sending bright young junior executives to the university for specialized training."

SECTION VII

ATTACKS ON BUSINESS—AND WHAT TO DO

LEMUEL BOULWARE, FORMER Vice President and a General Manager of General Electric sums up the attack on business and what can be done to correct misconceptions as follows:

"My thesis is two-fold:

"*First*, that private business investors and managers are now hitting a new low in dangerous misunderstanding and disapproval by most of the public. The charges of *brute, crook* and *exploiter*—put forward skillfully and relentlessly by the enemies of private business over a long period—have gone unrefuted so completely as to make business silence appear confession of guilt as charged. The safety of corporate investment and of other private property—and the usefulness of business to all the public—are imperiled as never before.

"*Second*, that business has ample help potentially available from the *inherently interested millions* of direct and indirect investors in business, but that this potential can be converted to *actual* help *only* by managers in company after company alerting, enlisting, equipping, and *constantly re-equipping and encouraging* those particular investors and other property owners whom the individual manager has opportunity to contact as shareowners, employees, suppliers, customers and neighbors.

"I realize such corrective work has not usually been considered a part of the manager's job. But I believe the situation is now so urgent that top management has to face two requirements: *First*, to fix any deficiencies about which the public dissatisfaction is warranted. *Second*, to correct the misinformation about the rest; fortunately, there is no need to attack the sources of this misinformation—just go after the so obviously bad arithmetic and bad morals involved.

"Owners and managers have been all too guilty of malfeasance through their inattention and silence making them a party to the public being misled into disassociating cause and effect . . . that is, a party to the public being

This shop was one hit by looters on 4/27/70 after violence spilled out on the streets following fighting between black and white students at River Rouge (Michigan) High School. Additional police were brought from other communities and officials imposed a 6 p.m. to 5 a.m. curfew.   UPI allowed to lose sight of the inevitably necessary one-to-one ratio between benefits daily desired and benefits that have to be daily produced.

"I submit that the obvious need for correcting this neglect is all around us now in the crisis we see mounting in our whole society—with special impact on private business. It is essentially a *crisis of false expectations*.

"All of us Americans seem freshly impatient to live a whole lot better right away. That is understandable—and we *can* readily do so, *provided* each citizen will really see and do his obligated part toward that end.

"But hard to understand—after all our much vaunted education at home, at school and at church—is that most of our fellow citizens so clearly demand and expect that *their take* will be *much greater* than *their contribution*. They seem to want too much too soon for too little in return . . . and thus want 'instant utopia' *too largely from someone else*. For there is the foolish belief that government, or private business, of future generations can and will somehow supply the difference now between what these citizens produce and what they want.

"Such impractical economic expectations—involving such distressing moral aberrations—are rooted mainly, I believe, in these three causes:

"1. The majority does not realize that *consumers pay all the expenses of any business that long survives;* that these expenses—including all wages and taxes—are paid in current prices, or in delayed progress in future values, or in both; and that most always even a strike over wages is not a conflict of interest between workers and owners but between workers and consumers among which latter are, of course, the workers themselves.

"2. The majority does not know that *individual* citizens, as tax-paying *consumers*, supply all the money government spends, regardless of whether this money is taken from consumers in direct taxes, or in the taxes government levies on business and then has business collect from consumers in prices, or in the tax of inflation arising from government's borrowing and then deceitfully counterfeiting under the pleasant name of 'monetizing debt.'

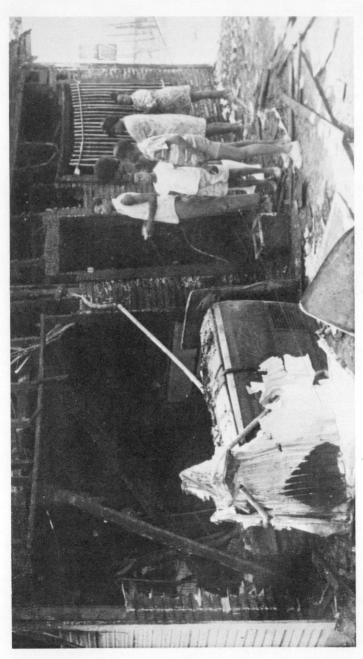

Negro children inspect the gutted white-owned grocery, which was destroyed after a firebomb was hurled through a window in Jackson, Mississippi on 5/21/70. The grocery, located in a predominantly Negro section, was the sixth report of firebomb attacks in Jackson since violence erupted the week before at Jackson State College.   UPI

"3. The majority does not recognize the obvious fact that we can and do have only what we produce; that the level of living can be raised only by us, as specialists, doing more for each other; and that it is naive as well as dishonest for the majority to go on putting its present heavy dependence on the economically pitiful and morally disgraceful idea of getting something-for-nothing *for the many* through gang force imposed on some *few* via the voting booth, the bargaining table, or privileged violence. . . ."

Is it not time for business, large and small, to undertake a massive, intelligent and effective educational campaign so that the public can get the truth about the free market? Or actively support such honest, legitimate and constructive efforts designed to do so?

SECTION VIII

MASS MEDIA MIND MANAGEMENT

WRITING IN THE November 1970 issue of *Christian Economics,* Clarence Manion, former Dean, College of Law at Notre Dame, brings an underlying cause of our turmoil into sharp focus. He Says:

"The brainwashing of an individual is blunt, brutal, physical and psychological torture tailored to fit the susceptibilities of the particular victim who is under the complete control of his captors. To subdue the mind of an entire nation calls for a much more prolonged and sophisticated system of disguised mental coercion. The complex, interlocked communications system in our country today, augmented by what has become an almost completely perverted educational system, could have been made to order by and for those amorphous forces that have now laid siege to the American mind. This interlocked system of sound, sight and the printed word facilitates what one learned psychologist has called the 'engineering of popular consent.'

"The real target of mass media mind management is in the political, social and behavioral attitudes of the American people. The important objective in mass mind management is social indoctrination. And without the shield of eternal vigilance, it is impossible for anybody in this country to avoid its impact today. . . .

"The mass mind managers know this. They do not waste their time or energies lobbying in Washington or the State Capitol. They work on the American mind, knowing full well that the politicians will follow the change in that mind with the instant interpretation and knee-jerk reaction that distinguishes success from failure in American politics. Thus, before you W-R-I-T-E your Congressman effectively, you must R-I-G-H-T yourself, your neighbors and your community and let your Congressman know that you have done so. In other words, you must work effectively to wake up and alert the presently benumbed and hypnotized American mind.

". . . The church has not merely relinquished its welfare services to the government of our new mass society; generally speaking the church has willfully walked away from its basic doctrinal anchorage, namely, the Ten Commandments, and deliberately traded its traditional concern for the enlightenment of the personal eternally responsible conscience for the preachment of social consciousness, social responsibility and relativistic situation ethics. . . .

ASSESSING AMERICA—"SUICIDE"

"For years, our most prestigious American universities have been pouring out authoritative statements that American society and its institutions are utterly undeserving of respect (*Wall Street Journal*, March 31, 1970). American parents complain that they cannot control their children; university presidents have no answer to S.D.S. blackmail except complete capitulation.

"What is wrong with America? Ask Castro's 1,000 American volunteer sugar-cane cutters; ask the 'Chicago Five'; ask the S.D.S.; ask Sam Brown who organized the anti-Vietnam War Mobilization Day last year and the Earth Day-Anti-Pollution Demonstration on Lenin's birthday this year.

THEIR ANSWER

"What is *their* answer? 'Everything is wrong with America; everything and anything that you can use as an excuse to destroy America; for instance, peace, poverty, pollution, exploding population. For peace, quit fighting the Communists; for poverty, confiscate and divide up all the property; for pollution, destroy American industries because they are the ones polluting the air and the water; for the population explosion, kill the unborn now and the useless old people later, empty all the nursing homes into the nearest cemetery. Burn the population candle at both ends, but do Burn, Baby, Burn everything. Destroy man, Destroy, Destroy.'

WHO? . . . ME?

"Now, ask the Silent Majority, 'What is wrong with America?' What do you hear now? Nothing. The majority is not just silent, the majority is asleep! This is the final destructive course of 'Suicide.' The majority has handed over its mind and its mouth to the public opinion engineers.

"Are you sick of seeing Jerry Rubin of the convicted Chicago Seven holding up his clenched Communist fist on your television screen? Then say so. Are you happy to know that Dave Dellinger and William Kuntsler, convict and sentenced counselor respectively, are lecturing regularly on all the big college campuses getting $1,000 and $2,000 for each appearance? What do you think these convicts are preaching to the students? Peace? Or riot, revolution and war? Do you think we can expect law observance and respect for life, liberty and property from a generation that has grown to manhood without hearing anything about God and the role of the Ten Commandments in producing a civilized society?

YOUTH—AFRAID OF REALITY?

"A Los Angeles psychiatrist has told *U.S. News and World Report* (April 27, 1970) that the trouble with our youth is that 'they are running away from reality.' The youth are not running away from reality. We have *withdrawn* them from reality—from the basic essential reality, namely, the Reality of God. Our youthful revolutionaries have surrendered to Communism's 'Almighty Man,' because we have let them grow up without the only adequate counter-challenge—Faith in Almighty God.

THE ONLY SOLUTION

"When our Apollo 13 astronauts appeared to be hopelessly lost in space, we prayed publicly for their safe return, and we were heard. Before the God's Truth that makes all men free is hopelessly lost in the demoralized atheistic thicket of 1984, let us pray, publicly, reverently, regularly, and *officially* for the return of faith in God to the United States.

"Whittaker Chambers, the disillusioned, heartbroken ex-Communist, reminded us that the history of the world is cluttered with the wreckage of nations that became indifferent to God. We can and must reverse this suicidal course."

THE TWO PLATOON SYSTEM

To achieve their goals the two platoon system is being actively employed by the Socialist revolutionary instigators. Semantics and double talk play an important part. For instance:

They preach orderly change—and encourage violent revolution;

They preach love—and practice hate;

They plead that the poor need money (bread)—but seek to destroy the wealth-producing system;

They shed tears for the over-burdened taxpayer—and call for bigger appropriations for more special groups;

They call for more individual freedom—and advocate more government force and coercion to solve all personal and social problems;

They want free speech—but deny it to others with "non-violent" obscenities;

They say they tell it "like it is"—and then employ double talk semantics to cover their real meaning;

They say let the courts interpret the present "living" constitution—but call for a new constitution to make the revolution a legal reality.

They talk of morality—and practice immorality.*

You can enlarge the list almost endlessly.

In this semantical tactical process, many well-meaning adults and idealistic youths are caught up by a small well-trained hard core of radicals and are innocently dragged into the stream flowing toward a completely Socialized America.

WHAT TO DO

The meaning of words has been so distorted and cleverly used that the true message the trained socialists use is completely different from what you *think* you hear, read or understand.

Therefore, the study of Socialist/Communese is a most important task for all to undertake. Otherwise, you may become a carrier of the socialist message unwittingly.

For that reason a brief Dictionary of Double Talk is included in this volume as a helpful tool.

SECTION IX

SEMANTICS AND THE REVOLUTION

J. EDGAR HOOVER says: ". . . Communists still use Aesopian language; they say one thing and mean another. In this manner, they fool non-Communists, encouraging them to believe that communism stands for something desirable . . ." Those who wonder why thousands of young people, and adults, will follow revolutionary leaders will find some answers in the clever, diabolic use of language.

*Note: Some officials are catching on to the "moral" semantics. For instance *The Washington Post*, March 20, 1971, reported that when a student leader demanded that students have the right to run the on-campus "co-educational" dorms, including round-the-clock visiting hours, The Chairman of the Board of Regents replied, "The University of Maryland is a place of education, not a ----house." The Regents rejected the demand.

Roy E. Colby, Semantics expert and Professor of Language at the University of Northern Colorado, has made a special study of this "revolutionary rhetoric." Recently, in a speech to members of the faculty at the University, he illustrated how revolutionary rhetoric is used today by quoting from a leaflet. The leaflet says at the bottom, "Excerpt from the Program of the Rocky Mountain Revolutionary Union, An End to R.O.T.C."

The leaflet states:

". . . The way the University complex best serves imperialism is exemplified in R.O.T.C. The chief confrontation taking place is between a world in revolution and amerikkkan imperialism. People are rising up to free themselves from amerikkkan corporate exploitation. They will no longer passively watch their human and natural resources exploited, their country's chance for economic growth stiffled [sic] by amerikkkan economic domination and be pacified with care [sic] packages.

"Amerikkkan imperialism is the main structure standing in the way of our brother's [sic] liberation. R.O.T.C. supplies over half of the officers for fragmentation bombs, defoileges [sic] and fires the guns all under the guise of fighting for democracy. It trains men in the tactics of counter-insurgency and gives them the manpower to protect and foster the goals of a dehumanizing corporate imperialism. We demand an immediate end to R.O.T.C. . . ."

"Read that over again," said Prof. Colby, "and note well certain words. (Never mind the spelling—What do you want, good spelling or revolution?) Look at them: University complex, imperialism, confrontation, revolution, amerikkkan imperialism, people, exploitation, exploited, economic domination, liberation, free (themselves), structure, under the guise of, and corporate imperialism.

"These words and others similar to them constitute revolutionary rhetoric, the vocabulary of revolution. They are all logical parts of a verbal pattern which is invariable in its make-up. Here are the elements which constitute the pattern.

"A revolution is a violent overthrow of a government and is usually abhorred by a majority of the people. How then do you arouse people, convince them the government should be overthrown?

"Very simply. *You say it is all bad.*

"Therefore, all the things you do and stand for are good.

"What do you attack?—*the sources of power.*

"What are the sources of power?

"The University. The Courts, The Police. The Armed Forces . . . .

"Revolutionary rhetoric is remarkable for the ideas it does not express. Nothing about the rights of the majority. Nothing about whether actions proposed lead to the greater freedom of the individual—not of a class or group of people, but of the individual citizen. Nothing good about America's great social progress in the last two decades. Nothing about the responsibilities connected with the exercise of constitutional rights. Nothing good about any non-Communist country. Nothing bad about any Socialist or Communist country.

"Please note this point. In revolutionary rhetoric, the government is held responsible for the welfare of the citizens and hence for all the nation's ills. The individuals who comprise our people-run society somehow are held blameless—except the President of the United States. Since, then, the government is not attending to the country's needs, or not doing it fast enough, the *government should be destroyed*.

"Simplistic reasoning? Perhaps so, but too many of our students are falling for it. We, as educators, ought to have some responsibility for the views of our students. What has gone wrong in education when twice as many students believe the government is doing a bad job as those believing it is doing well?

"We must come up with ways and means to cope with revolutionary rhetoric and the superficial ideas that lie behind it. If we don't—let each draw his own conclusion . . ."

It is clear that one of the imperatives is: Everyone, especially students, teachers and parents must learn to understand what revolutionary rhetoric means. That's why a brief *Dictionary* of *Double Talk*, compiled by Prof. Colby, is included in this book.

SECTION X

MANY CHURCHES A PART OF THE PROBLEM

MANY CHURCH BODIES have, as Dean Manion says, become part of the problem and are contributing to the socialist revolution. They do so by dignifying Godless communism, teaching its theory and practice as though it is desirable and by compromising with anarchists.

One example illustrates the point. Dr. John C. Bennett, former President of Union Theological Seminary, New York, and now at the Graduate Theological Union in Berkeley, California, wrote in the August 3, 1970, issue of *Christianity and Crisis* as follows:

> "First, the time has come to free ourselves from the combination of residual national messianism and anti-communist crusading. Our more thoughtful readers know that this whole picture of an international Communist movement that threatens the 'free world' from many sides is out-of-date. We should abandon the idea that there is a worldwide communism that constitutes a unified threat and is, by definition, the greatest evil that can befall any country regardless of the alternatives. Who are we to say that communism may not be better for some nations than generations of stagnation in poverty, than decades of civil war, than a rightist tyranny that cares nothing about the welfare of the people? It would be a rational policy to allow various kinds of communism to find their own level . . ."

Isn't it strange that ministers are being trained to discontinue the fight against Godless communism at the very time when we are in the midst of a socialist-Marxist revolution?

THE SOCIAL GOSPEL AND THE
LIBERAL ESTABLISHMENT

Dr. James DeForest Murch in *The Protestant Revolt* makes the case rather explicit. He writes:

> "The Social Gospel is little more nor less than Socialism. It calls for public ownership of all significant sectors of

public life, such as banking, transportation and communications. In practice, it means the government ownership of the major means of production with consequent power to dispose of the fruits of labor. It means the cancellation of plans and programs which have been developed by individual and corporate incentive, the establishment of new quotas for factories, fields and mines, assignment of jobs, fixing of wages and hours of labor and the terms under which they may exchange. A few men exercising inordinate political power will then ride herd on the masses. The individual will no longer be permitted to exercise his God-given rights. . .

"All of which means that the Liberal Establishment in effect is committed to the following objectives: (1) The scrapping of the profit motive, (2) the elimination of competition and the creation of a system of cooperation which will allow for government planning, (3) the placing of all natural resources under public ownership and control, (4) 'cooperation' in economic life through state planning, and (5) a softening of our relationships with communist states.

"The tragic thing about Protestantism's growing abdication of its moral and spiritual sovereignty and its concern for the salvation of the individual is that modern society is now plunging into what promises to be the greatest moral debacle in history. With all the church's talk about the Kingdom of God on earth, America is in an advanced state of moral decline which, if continued, will lead inevitably to the 'City of Decay' and the 'Valley of Doom.' The Liberal Establishment is advocating lawlessness in the arena of civil rights; treating crime as a disease and not as sin; protecting the rights of criminals and disregarding the plight of their victims; destroying individual responsibility in favor of social consensus; and accepting economic and political corruption as justifiable means for the advancement of good ends. Never has the line between good and evil been as blurred and indistinct as it is today. Never has America been nearer destruction. . ."

Isn't it time for church members to take a look at what their church gifts are being used for?

Have we forgotten that our great nation was built on Christian principles?

Or, is the term misunderstood?

The Jewish writer, George Sokolsky, twenty years ago wrote a description that should be helpful to all:

"We speak of ours as a Christian civilization. But among us live some 50 races of man and some 250 religious groups, many of which are not Christian. And they should take no umbrage that we call ours a Christian civilization. Jews, Moslems, Buddhists, Confucians—all the non-Christians among us, realizing that men and women of good will respect their concepts of God and faith—must also recognize that in this year, 1951 years after the date accepted as the birth of Jesus, the great struggle is between God and the Devil, between Good and Evil, between Christianity and Marxism."

And isn't it appropriate to ask those who are contributing millions in support of seminaries to ask, "What are you teaching?" Should my money be used to destroy the very system of morals, self-government, and free enterprise that has built America—and has given me and millions opportunity and freedom?"

". . . It must also be remembered "writes Clare Boothe Luce in the *Honolulu* magazine," that millions of youths who have entered college in the past five years were the sons and daughters of parents who had not gone to college. Many of these 'first generation' students literally did not know how to behave in the 'Halls of Reason.' Many of their ideas of Free Speech and Protest, for example, were inherited from fathers who were better acquainted with the rhetoric of the hiring-hall and the manners of the picketline than with the traditional rehtoric and manners of Academia. . ."

Hence, it is essential that every patriotic American understand: WHO is behind the revolution? and WHAT are their goals? We must also learn to recognize their tactics and strategy whether employed by the innocent, by the duped or the trained socialist or Marxist.

WHO IS TO BLAME?

Edumnd A. Opitz, also in *The Protestant Revolt*, writes:

". . . Christians have always felt an obligation to improve the natural and social orders, but they have never

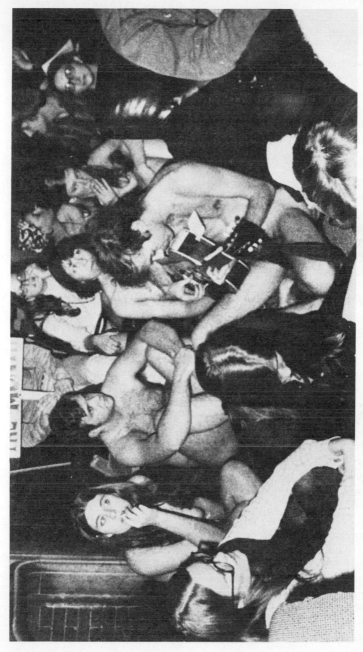

Grinnell College Students, on 2/5/69, disrobe in a protest to *Playboy* Magazine's philosophy during a speech by *Playboy* representative, Bruce Draper, in Grinnell, Iowa. The demonstrators said they were members of the Grinnell Women's Liberation group and the Guerrilla Theater. The latter sponsored a male homecoming queen, the former concentrates on birth control information.   UPI

until now equated a perfected social order with the Kingdom of God. This Kingdom was regarded as another
dimension of existence, another realm of being, not simply
an extension of our present set-up. But the late Bishop G.
Bromley Oxnam told the Fifth World Order Study Conference in 1958 that Christians should 'so change the
planet that when our first visitors from Mars arrive they
will find a society fit to be called the Kingdom of God.'. . .

SECOND CLASS CITIZENSHIP FOR DISSENTERS

"Besides being uneconomic, the Liberal program is also
unjust. The rationale for the Welfare State is: Somebody's
program at everybody's expense. The great mass of people
have not been converted to Liberal orthodoxy in economic
and political matters; they are unbelievers, and so they
must be punished for holding beliefs deemed to be incorrect. Of course, these present-day heretics are not burned at
the stake, but neither were most heretics during the Ages
of Faith. Most heretics then merely suffered confiscation
of property and certain civil disabilities—just as today.
Those whose convictions do not permit them to endorse
Social Security, Urban Renewal, Foreign Aid, and all the
rest are nevertheless forced to help pay for these projects.
A portion of their income and property is taxed away
from Conservatives and Libertarians and used to further
the Liberal program, which is that much less these people
have for their own programs. Dissenters from the Liberal
Creed do not have equality of rights with those in power.
If this kind of thing were occurring in the religious realm
everyone would acknowledge a serious breach of religious
liberty; it is no less serious as a breach of civil liberty.
Liberalism generates a body of second-class citizens as an
intrinsic part of its operation.

"These are some of the features of the thing which has
emerged in our midst. If we don't like them we have no
one to blame but ourselves, laymen and clergymen alike.
The Church is people; not other people, us! During the
course of the past several generations things have been
done that should not have been done, while other things
have been left undone. There has been indifference, sloth,
preoccupation with other concerns. Defections have created a vacuum, so to speak, into which dubious ideologies

have seeped. These ideologies have found embodiment in people and programs, and together they constitute the challenge we face. Part time or half-hearted resistance will not avail; the effort must be a heroic one, for, as Edmund Burke wrote, 'When once things are gone out of their ordinary course, it is by acts out of the ordinary course they can alone be reestablished.' With God's help, we may make it!..."

SECTION XI

CITIZEN'S ROLE IN SECURING PROPER CHANGE

RECENTLY, THE Citizens Evaluation Institute received a letter from a person who identified himself as an engineer. In it he wrote:

"... As a democratic socialist, I reject the use of violence by agitators of the right or left as long as we retain the democratic alternative..."

This letter personalizes the widespread generalized propaganda promoting any *change* if it is arrived at "democratically"; i.e., peacefully. That is the program of the less militant democratic socialists.

We may well confront those who say they *deplore change by VIOLENCE but are for "orderly" PEACEFUL CHANGE* and ask them, for instance:

What do you want to get by orderly peaceful change?

Do you want to improve the system of constitutional, local, self-government that protects private property, as envisioned by the Founders of this Republic, *or* do you want change that moves us further toward taking from the producers to give to the non-producers by governmental power?

Do you want CHANGE that improves the free-choice market system *or* CHANGE that destroys it by including more government planning, spending regulation, taxation, and intervention?

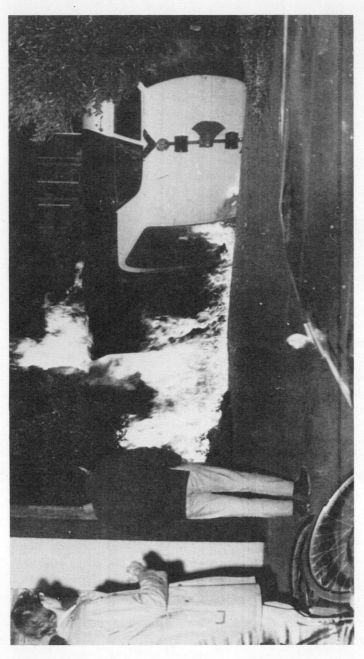

A police car burns after being set afire by rampaging demonstrators protesting the "Chicago Seven" riot trial. Some one thousand demonstrators, many from the University of California at Santa Barbara smashed windows, set fires and threw rocks and bottles at police during the rampage on February 25, 1970. UPI

Do you want CHANGE that strengthens the character of man based on Judeo-Christian ethics? *or* CHANGE to create a completely permissive, atheistic, immoral order?

Do you want more CHANGE in educational institutions to make them honest institutions of learning? *or* CHANGE that makes them centers of revolution?

Do you want CHANGE in higher education to strengthen it as a privilege for those who want to learn? *or* CHANGE to make attendance a matter of right regardless of motivation, attitude, competence, or behavior?

Unless we are clear on what specific propositions will do TO people—not just FOR them—what it will do TO a free choice economic system—not just FOR it—what it will do TO constitutional local self-government in this Republic—not just FOR it, it is easy to innocently move toward the revolutionary's goal . . . a complete socialist state.

Unfortunately, Americans do not object to the term "Socialism" today as strongly as they did in the early part of the century. Even Marxism has become respectable in some classrooms and in the political arena. Mass mind management has been effective. We have been softened up!

The formula that the Socialists devised early in this century has been effective and is still being employed. Namely: *Be prepared to compromise in order to move from where the opponents (Patriotic Americans) are to where we (Socialists) want to go—and we (the Socialists) will always win.*

Hence, the principle of the *inevitability of gradualism* is their guiding star. This is their political process of compromising with evil. This is "peaceful change" according to them.

But the result—Socialism—can be achieved by peaceful gradualism just as it can with violent revolution.

Since we have already adopted a large degree of socialism, including a redistribution of wealth through graduated taxation, many citizens are lulled to inactivity when more is proposed under the various banners of—welfare—or—aid to education—or—a job for all—or—guaranteed income—or—national health insurance—or—granting this or that wish as a matter of right.

Citizens need to know WHO the planners are NOW. WHAT their real goals are NOW. WHERE the action is NOW. WHY we are not getting the truth NOW.

". . . Socialism "says Clare Boothe Luce," gains its most recruits among students who decide to work in the welfare sector of government. . ."

We must recognize that the academic community is not alone in teaching a Socialist form of government, or glorifying a "new life style." Other professions like medicine, law, and religion also have their "teachers of destruction." It appears that the military, police, and other security forces and the judicial system also have been penetrated with their "teachers" and "activists." And the business and industrial fields are not immune. Music with its rock and roll and the arts with various forms of pornography are part of the destructive process.

The financing of this revolution comes largely from certain business and religious sources—perhaps with the hope that they will get their share of the spoils in the resulting totalitarian-socialist order. But the taxpayer, through government programs, is also paying a price. We need to keep in mind that "who shall rule" is at stake in any struggle of this magnitude.

SECTION XII

THERE IS HOPE . . . WITH WORK

SOME COLLEGE ADMINISTRATORS have acted to retain their schools as institutions of learning. Others are beginning to. Most college professors have not been in sympathy with the destructive Socialist teachers. A few in an organized way and others as individuals are beginning to assert themselves.

Consider, for example, James M. Buchanan, Professor of Economics and General Director for the Center for Public Choice, Virginia Polytechnic Institute. In a speech to Phi Kappa Phi, a scholastic honor society, he said:

". . . Consider . . . the standard academic attitude toward student violence. This attitude which may, unfortunately, be held by a large majority of the academic community, deplores the resort to violence by student-faculty militants. But it involves the strong opposition to any reaction to violence or threats thereof by university authorities. The attitude supports appeasement in almost all circumstances. When militants stone policemen, when they occupy or burn buildings—these are considered unfortunate, but there is widespread sentiment against effective disciplinary action. And if such steps are taken, there arises a general cry for amnesty. The expressed feeling that if only militants are treated nicely after they have burned one or two buildings maybe they will then be good boys and not burn any more . . .

"Consider . . . the naiveté of those who expect the American taxpayer to continue to finance education in chaos. If student strikes do not harm the students who are the supposed beneficiaries of education, then by their own admission education is worthless. If education is worthless to the student, then why should the taxpayer finance our salaries to provide something on which consumers themselves place a zero value? This much could be said even if there were no more. But there is more. Why should the taxpayer, either directly or indirectly, finance universities and colleges when he sees that their products are devoted to overthrowing the very society that nourishes them? These are the questions that the taxpayers are quite properly asking. We have seen this happen in many states where bond and tax proposals have been defeated in referenda. The squeeze is already on higher education in California, in Wisconsin, in Ohio, in Indiana, and in several other states . . .

"How can we, as members of the academic community, be honest with ourselves in demanding that the taxpayer finance the barbaric invasion of the lawn in Charlottesville, correctly described as the most beautiful enclosure of space in the world? How can we honestly ask the Virginia taxpayer to finance a university that allows itself to become politicized? How can we ask the taxpayer to support the education of students who occupy buildings, block major traffic arteries, and disrupt normal educational processes? The answer is that we cannot. To do so would clearly be fraudulent ... Yet most academic personnel would be aghast at my statements here. They feel, for some strange reason, that the academicians are God's chosen people in the modern world, and that the taxpayer should continue to throw his money over the ivy wall, so to speak, that it is boorish for him to so much as inquire as to what goes on behind those walls. The modern academician seems in this respect as in others to have lost elementary common sense. Hopefully, there are some among us who can recognize such folly. We must acknowledge, and welcome, the taxpayers' role. Through their political representatives, the taxpayers must begin to distinguish between those educational programs which serve their traditional social purpose and those that do not ... "

THERE IS HOPE—A FEW EXAMPLES

Stanford University (Calif.) President Richard W. Lyman summarily relieved young activist Professor Howard Bruce Franklin of his teaching duties on Feb. 12, 1971 for his alleged "important role" in two anti-war demonstrations the week before.

Professor Franklin called for a "people's war" against the Santa Clara County sheriff's deputies and San Jose Police who were patrolling the campus following a takeover of the university's computer center by student radicals.

The president asked for a faculty hearing board to dismiss Prof. Franklin. The courts also issued a temporary restraining order to prevent the professor and 16 others from committing "destructive or disruptive acts at the university."

Perhaps other presidents will begin to follow Mrs. Luce's recommendation by dismissing professors who engage in disruptive activities. (see Section II)

There are, of course, hundreds of others who have acted firmly or spoken out.

Dr. Ernest L. Wilkinson, the president of Brigham Young University (Utah), made the rules and policies of the University clear to both students and their parents. He did so in writing as well as by speeches and face-to-face discussion. In essence he said, "If you want to learn and can live by our policies, we will be glad to have you. If not, don't enroll, or leave if you are here."

As reported by James J. Kilpatrick in *The Washington Star*, Nathan M. Pusey [then president] of Harvard,* in his spring 1970 baccalaureate said, "Some faculty, who for reasons not quite clear to me, would like to see our colleges and universities denigrated, maligned, and even shut down . . . It is a shameful state of affairs . . ." He went on to speak of these militants and their techniques in words that cracked like whips: hateful, cunning, deceitful, ignorant, intolerant, sickening. He closed with his own confession of error. "The inroads into academic life could not have grown so deep," he said, "had all of us to whom they are deeply repulsive been more ready to oppose them."

Philip B. Kurland, professor of law at the University of Chicago, spoke to the Women's Bar Association of Illinois on June 4, 1970. Among his remarks was this firm and logical statement:

"The essence of the academy is disinterestedness. Its justification is disinterestedness. A university cannot be both a political force and an institution dedicated to the search for knowledge and its dissemination. As a university makes a political commitment it destroys its claim to academic freedom. And without academic freedom, the search for the dissemination of knowledge becomes more shadow than substance.

"In the caretaker institutions of the future, answers will be substituted for questions, and indoctrination will replace education."

This is the price, he said, "that America will pay for the cowardice of its university faculties."

And Gardner Ackley, professor of Economics at the University of Michigan, in a speech early in 1970 was just as positive and heartening. He pointed out that, "The past academic year has taught the lesson," he said, "that violence and disruption either cannot or will not be punished by the university." He pointed out that striking teachers are not

*The new president, Derek Curtis Bok, is expected to be a compromiser and reformer. His past performance indicates that he will accede to student demands.

punished; they are reappointed. Student vandals are not expelled; they are retained.

Then he continued. "Last Wednesday I watched the faculty of my own department assembled in the chairman's office, discuss a demand that all classes in our building be shut down, or else. We discussed this while the entrances to the building were sealed and while the halls outside the rooms in which we were meeting were patrolled by men carrying pipes and clubs. We sought guidance from the college and were told: 'Do what you think best; you will have no protection.' And so we cravenly capitulated, in fear—if not for our own safety—for that of our students and employees. That day the truth lay in those clubs."

CONCERNED SCHOLARS ORGANIZE

Perhaps one of the greatest hopes for strengthening the colleges and universities as "centers of learning" rather than all becoming "centers of revolution" lies in the recent grass roots formation of the University Professors for Academic Order, Inc. Dr. Z. Michael Szaz, American Institute on Problems of European Unity, is Executive Director.

U.P.A.O. is committed to take concrete and positive actions to prevent the increasing politicization and the ideological takeover of the institutions of American higher education by radical faculty members, students and outsiders whose early symptoms are the continuing purge of "nonconformist" faculty members.

On January 31, 1971 the organization adopted several important statements of policy. Among them are: "A university should not permit a minority acting in concert to infringe upon the rights of the majority of the academic community." Another one is: "Should the conviction of a professor so acutely conflict with the freedom he has earned that he finds them incompatible with the simultaneous fulfillment of his contractual obligations as a faculty member, he should either request a leave of absence or resign."

Although newly organized in 1970, it already has chapters or members on 290 campuses. Dr. Justus van der Kroef, Uni-

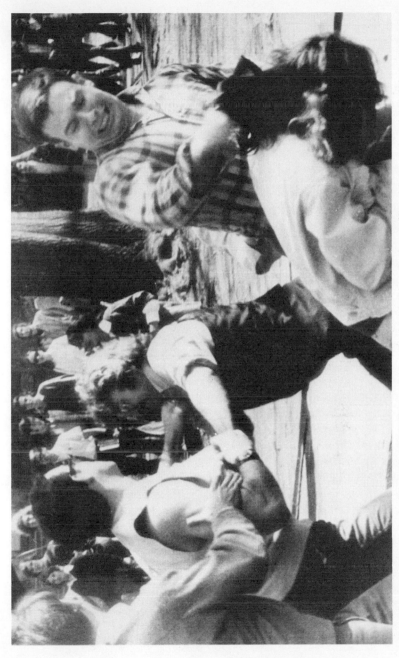

Two University of North Carolina (Chapel Hill) students with conservative hair cuts scuffle with two long-haired UNC students over a march of the "long-hairs" carrying a North Vietnam flag. The march was part of a protest of the "Chicago Seven" trial. UPI

versity of Bridgeport, was elected President on January 15, 1971.

Several members of the Board of Scholars, CEI, hold important positions in the organization as follows: Dr. Anthony T. Bouscaren, Le Moyne College, and Professor Roy E. Colby, University of Northern Colorado, are members of the Board of Directors; and Dr. Jerzy Hauptmann, Park College, is Chairman of the Committee on University Teaching and Research, and Chairman, Region V.

WHY ARE THERE CRISES IN THE COLLEGES?

It may be that the financial crises that many colleges and universities are now facing result at least partially from the reluctance of taxpayers and donors from supporting institutions because the customers (students) have placed, by the minority action, a low value on the product (education) they are getting.

Could it be that sensible people see the folly of such theories as

(a) Everybody is *entitled* to a college education?
(b) Everybody *should* go to college?
(c) Everyone who goes should get a *degree*?
(d) Admission standards are *not required*?
(e) Class attendance is *not required*?
(f) Examinations are *not required*?
(g) Hiring and firing of faculty *should rest with the students*?
(h) Students should *outline courses of study*?
(i) Colleges should be *centers of revolution*?
(j) Professors *cannot be dismissed* even though they advocate revolution, anarchy, communism or other political dogma that would destroy the American system?
(k) Colleges should involve themselves in *community and national politics*?

Have you examined your college, university, seminary and high school curricula, books, programs and faculty?

TAXPAYERS FOOT THE BILL

While the taxpayer needs to examine the kind of academic institutions he is supporting, he cannot stop there.

He must also examine laws, government programs and policies which his representatives have passed—and he is supporting.

One key question is: Are they leading us further down the road to Socialism, *silently*?

Recent developments highlight this problem in a new way. This can be illustrated by projects included in the government's various so-called anti-poverty programs. A case in point is one supposedly providing funds for legal services to the poor.

In their syndicated column, in *The Washington Post,* November 1970, Rowland Evans and Robert Novak, reported a case illustrating how such funds may have been used.

For instance, police raided the National Committee to Combat Fascism, a Black Panther front, on September 15, 1970 in New Orleans. The NCCF specializes in police-baiting.

Present was Robert Glass, a lawyer, allegedly employed by the federally funded New Orleans Legal Assistance Corporation (part of the anti-poverty program). When police asked him questions, he invoked his client-lawyer relationship excuse. Subsequently, 12 NCCF members charged with attempted murder, assault and other felonies, were represented by NOLAC lawyers. Not all the facts surrounding this case are known. Neither are the facts known for thousands of other cases which are "defended" by taxpayers' money.

WILL THE TRUTH COME OUT?

Recently Governor Ronald Reagan itemized a series of charges against the California Rural Legal Assistance Program in connection with his veto of a federal appropriation for this "class action agency." A liberal subcommittee of the Senate insisted that the veto be overridden by the Administration.

Instead, a grant for extending the program six months was approved. It carried a proviso that a Presidential Commission be appointed to investigate the charges. A review was to begin on February 1, 1971.

Since the members of the Commission are not known at the time of this writing, it is difficult to predict the outcome. However, if the reports of previous Presidential Commission reports (student unrest, violence, pornography, etc.) is any guide, it will be surprising if the real nature of this costly program, of dubious constitutionality, will be uncovered by it.

QUESTIONS THAT DESERVE ASKING

Is the taxpayer supporting his own destruction by *violence* through payment of legal fees to protect the anarchists?

How widespread and in how many ways is the taxpayer footing the bill to destroy the American system?

How deep have the anarchists penetrated the legislative, judicial and administrative branches of government?

Is the technique of threatened blackmail kidnapping and torture of officials to become the condoned practice for raids on the Treasury or release of prisoners?

Should colleges and universities that teach or condone the destruction of the American system continue to get the benefit of tax-exemption?

Must the hardworking taxpayer support the shiftless, the lazy, the criminal, the drug addict - - - -?

Has "sharing-the-wealth" — once the whipping-stick slogan aimed at the wealthy—become the "bust program" in which all above the so-called poverty line must contribute to the establishment of a Socialist system in the U.S.A. by the force of government coercion?

How much violation of the Constitution will the taxpayer endure?

Richard Wilson, the nationally respected *Register and Tribune* (Des Moines) syndicated columnist, writing on Dec. 21, 1970, sheds some very disturbing light on these crucial questions. He reports:

". . . LSP—the legal services program of the Office of Economic Opportunity—has a caseload of more than one million in the courts and its cost [to the taxpayer] is equal to half that of running the entire federal court system.

"Thousands of well-meaning and not so well-meaning, lawyers, most of them young, operate through 260-odd legal services programs to protect and promote the rights of the poor. They are creating a new and complex body of law.

"Sounds good, doesn't it? The poor are at last being protected from rapacious landlords, price gougers, venal officials, fraudulent operators.

"Stop right there. Among the clients of LSP lawyers are pornographers, rebellious students, hippies, Black Panthers and boys who don't want their hair cut. Proclaimed the former head of the New Orleans office, Richard Buckley: *'Legal services exist for the redistribution of wealth and power.' [emphasis added.]*

"The idea now comes through a little stronger. What started as a service to give the poor justifiable protection through the good offices of public-spirited lawyers now is being used as an agency for the promotion of radicalism. In its muddleheaded way, the American Bar Association has lent itself to the cause on various transparent pretexts without recognizing, as it so often does not, its basic responsibilities . . .

"In too many instances, LSP has become a vehicle to support the life-style of young William B. Kunstlers breaking from their suburban inhibitions to go into the ghettoes and hippie communities in search of a *cause celèbre* and the benighted state of the new consciousness.

"Poverty has very little to do with it for too many of these crusaders. As Buckley so aptly put it: 'People trying to make changes in society are busted [arrested]. They're charged in criminal court. The congressional act [defense of those indicted for criminal acts] is a farce.'

"These putative Kunstlers wish to get right down to the causes of poverty—like too many other people being too rich, like corporations, farmers and railroads getting subsidies. It's no use fooling around with slum landlords. Go direct to headquarters and move against government officials and mortgage bankers.

"The result of this kind of thinking was that in New Orleans, to take the worst example, 27 percent of all liti-

. . . just doing our thing!

"I'll run over and pick up my unemployment check and then drop off at the University to see what's holding up my Federal Education Grant check and look into my Research Grant check."

"You go over to the free VD Clinic and check on your tests. On the way, farm out the kids at the free day school. Then go to the free Health Center and pick up my free glasses. After that, pick up our Food Stamps, and we'll meet at the Federal Building for mass protest against *The Stinking Establishment*."

gated cases were on behalf of those under criminal indictment, and wholly contrary to the letter and spirit of the statute setting up LSP. That ought to interest the Justice Department . . ."

This is an example showing what some columnists, some reporters and some newspapers are doing to expose some dangerous programs already on the books.

There is further hope.

Edmund A. Opitz, writing in the December 1970 issue of *The Freeman*, puts the reason for hope in another way as follows:

THE INHERENT STABILITY OF THE MASSES

"There's something else below the surface of today's events, ready to be engaged in our cause, and that is the solid core of decency and common sense in the mass of men, covered over now and again, confused, but waiting to be enlisted. One often hears the despairing question, How can we win the masses back from liberalism? That's not our problem; the masses have never been converted *to* liberalism! To become a real liberal you have to go to graduate school! The average man, the man in the street, is not our problem. He may be mean, shiftless, ignorant, and a wife-beater when drunk, but he is not a collectivist and he is here by the millions, waiting to pin his emotions alongside the flag and cheer for the home team. Cardinal Newman was right: 'There is always in the multitude an acknowledgement of truths which they themselves do not practice.' When our side gets good enough, the multitudes will swarm in our direction.

"We have a real mess on our hands, but no one can say it is not richly deserved. For the past couple of centuries we have bullheadedly made a wrong choice at every opportunity. We have discarded the tried and true and let ourselves be seduced by the myths of an imminent utopia. We have embraced phony values and followed phony leaders. And in consequence of our folly things are in a bad way, but not as bad as they might be. Things aren't as bad as they would be if Reality were neutral. It is our great good fortune that the nature of things is on our side, on the side of freedom, that is; and it's the collectivists' tough luck that their program goes against the grain. There are forces in us and in the universe which make for growth and cohesion; unobstructed they make for liberty. Let's join 'em!"

EPILOGUE

In order that those seriously concerned with our crises today may dig deeper into this whole subject or acquire a better perspective of the problem, we have included several additional features in this document:

1. A brief Dictionary of Double Talk (Socialist/Communese—English) by Professor Roy E. Colby. With its use, you may learn what the trained Socialists really mean when they speak, preach, or write—and how the uninformed may innocently become part of their propaganda transmission belt.

2. A Bibliography of Suggested Reading for further study. This could be an endless list. However, the few selected books and periodicals listed will be helpful to those who wish to expand their understanding and be better prepared to take action.

3. A list of campus speakers and honoraria (from a Report, Committee on Internal Security, U.S. House of Representatives).

4. A few pictures to illustrate the kind of tactics used to induce violence and some consequences.

We suggest also that you read a recent statement by J. Edgar Hoover, Director of the Federal Bureau of Investigation, included as an EPILOGUE in *Teachers of Destruction*. In it, Mr. Hoover addresses himself to the need for certain corrective action that college administrators and law enforcement officers should take.

His statement may stimulate you to make a list of other corrective steps that should be taken. Such steps should be taken not only in the academic community (including rapid removal of faculty members who teach or encourage revolution and the examination of the tenure system) but also corrective action should be taken by responsible citizens in government, the courts, military, police, media, law, and medicine.

And most important is any action that will result in bringing the facts to the loyal American citizen. Perhaps when Americans realize that their tax burden is approaching that of the Socialist countries—Sweden, Norway, Denmark, England—and for the same reason—*Socialized government programs*—and that more are on the drawing boards—they may become vocal and act.

THE LOYAL AMERICANS AND THE EMERGING NEW GENERATION ARE TOMORROW'S HOPE — AND OUR PRESENT CONCERN.

March 1971

PART II

A Brief
DICTIONARY OF DOUBLE TALK
Socialist/Communese-English

By

ROY E. COLBY

. . . Communists still use Aesopian language; they say one thing and mean another. In this manner they fool non-communists, encouraging them to believe that communism stands for something desirable. The trained communist knows otherwise; it is more double talk with a completely different meaning. . . .

. . . Communism, in brief, has bitterly indicted communism; communist practice has indicted communist theory; communist actions have indicted the perverted use of such lofty words as "peace", "justice" and "liberty." . . .

. . . They clothe themselves with everything good, noble and inspiring to exploit these ideals to their own advantage. . . .

J. EDGAR HOOVER
in *Masters of Deceit*

More about
The Author

Roy Edward Colby brings a rich background of education and experience to bear in this Dictionary of Double Talk.

As a Foreign Service officer in the American Embassy in Havana, he saw Castro's Cuba develop before his eyes. He witnessed the daily unfolding of the master plan in which the entire communications system was used to achieve Socialist-Communist goals.

Prof. Colby served as an intelligence officer in World War II in Morocco, Algeria and Italy. Following nine years as an official in the International Educational Exchange Service, Department of State (1946-55), Prof. Colby spent the next seven years in the U.S. Foreign Service in Brazil, Mexico and Cuba. He was forced to leave on a few days notice when Castro came to power in 1961. Prof. Colby, a semantics expert, has been teaching language at the University of Northern Colorado at Greeley since 1962.

He has done research in the comparison of various aspects of Western and revolutionary semantics, ethics and logic. He is author of CONQUEST WITH WORDS.

His articles have appeared in *U.S. News & World Report, Rally Magazine, Elks Magazine, The New Guard* and *Human Events.*

Prof. Colby holds B.A. and M.A. degrees from Ohio University, *Magna cum Laude,* Phi Beta Kappa, and a M.A. Degree in Romance Languages, University of Michigan.

He is a member, Board of Directors, University Professors for Academic Order; and Board of Scholars, The Citizens Evaluation Institute. He is active in many civic affairs.

FOREWORD

Roy Colby

J. Edgar Hoover says ". . .Communists. . .say one thing and mean another. In this manner they fool non-communists, encouraging them to believe that communism stands for something desirable. . ."

Professor Roy Colby, a political semanticist at the University of Northern Colorado, has compiled a Glossary of Communist Terminology in *Conquest With Words*, defining the ideological meanings attached to Western words since 1935. Based on this Glossary and his *Communese-English Dictionary* now under preparation, he has selected the following list of words and expressions as an important part of *Revolutionary Actions. . .U.S.A. In Retrospect*.

It may be useful to readers who wish to understand the real meaning of some of the revolutionary statements and collectivist programs being presented to high school and college students by Socialist professors. Some well-trained "teachers" know exactly what is meant while others, not being aware of the ideological connotations, become unwitting carriers of the Socialist-Communist message.

As can be seen, these terms, along with hundreds of others, have secondary meanings, often distorted, unrelated and even opposite to their ordinary sense. They make up part of the ideo-political lingo of pseudo-liberalism, Socialism and Communism—Socialist/Communese.

INTRODUCTION

SOCIALIST/COMMUNESE —
LANGUAGE OF REVOLUTION

Here in America the *social revolution* is in full swing. Almost daily we witness mass physical actions, often involving violence, to pressure the *Establishment* into granting the *demands* of special interest groups. We see *peace marches* and *anti-war demonstrations*. The *military-industrial complex* is charged with syphoning off funds for an *unjust* and *immoral war* in Southeast Asia that could be used for *social* needs at home. We hear angry clamors for *restructuring* our universities and even our society itself. There are strident outcries against the *denial* of the *constitutional, civil* and *human rights* of *oppressed* minorities, and against *police brutality* and *repression*. Acts of terrorism and anarchy in the name of *social justice* are becoming increasingly more frequent throughout the land.

Slogans call for *peace, liberation, equality* and a *fair share* for all, and an end to *imperialism, oppression, racism* and *criminal discrimination. Liberals* and *progressives* even accuse *reactionaries* of *sexism*. Black, brown, red, white, *student* and female *militants*, among others, break laws and then arm themselves in *self-defense* against the *harassment, persecution, repression, overreaction* and *brutality* of the civil authorities. *The System* is blamed for having become a *police state* employing *Gestapo tactics* to stifle *free speech* and the *right* of *peaceful assembly*. The efforts of the *extremists* to curb pornography or subversion are branded as *hate literature* or infringement on the *right of free speech*.

Is this the America we know and love? No, it is not. It is the Socialist/Communese version of America. Are Americans aware that the italicized words and phrases in the two paragraphs above have special socio-political meanings to the revolutionaries who use them and correspond to their conception of reality and not ours? Probably not.

On the international scene, Communist propaganda floods us with strange applications of familiar terms of international law and diplomacy. We are told that our defense of South

Vietnam is really *aggression*, that the North Vietnamese attempt to conquer the country is *liberation*, and that the only way to achieve *peace* in Southeast Asia is through the withdrawal of U.S. troops. A *cease-fire* or *truce* in the Middle East turns out to be a means of reinforcing Soviet-Egyptian defenses along the Suez Canal, and of otherwise gaining strength. *Pravda* tells us the West German-Soviet *nonaggression treaty* is a praiseworthy step toward *lessening international tensions* in Western Europe. U.S. *imperialism* is bitterly denounced while Soviet *internationalism* is praised to the high heavens.

What goes on here? Do Americans realize the italicized terms have special ideo-political meanings to the purveyors of international revolution and don't correspond to the Western view of reality? Probably not.

This is the language of revolution. It is called Socialist/Communese and, when it is vocalized in English, a dictionary is needed to render it into understandable terms.

A UNIQUE KIND OF DICTIONARY

A Socialist/Communese—English Dictionary is unique, because it deals with a "foreign" language expressed in the English language. The practice of revolutionaries, especially the Communists and Socialists, of assigning ideological meanings to words makes it possible for any idea or judgment to have two distinct and often contradictory meanings: (1) the normal sense, i.e., standard English, and (2) the ideological sense, i.e., Socialist/Communese. It is double talk. Hence, the need for a dictionary to aid in converting, or actually translating, the ideological sense into everyday English that John Q. Public can understand.

WHO USES SOCIALIST/COMMUNESE?

Socialist/Communese expresses the thoughts and judgments of those persons, groups and nations that, for whatever reason, advocate immediate radical changes in the structure of Western society, that is to say, that promote the cause of social and political revolution. Socialist/Communese, then, is the communications medium not only of international Communism but also of pseudo-liberalism, of militancy, of the New Left, of collectivism, of Socialism, and of socio-political expediency in general.

Although Socialist/Communese is the official language of Moscow, Peking, Hanoi and Havana, it is also employed in the United Nations, in the halls of the U.S. Congress, in high school and college social studies classes and at campus demonstrations, in the pseudo-liberal press, and on protest signs in the streets. It is, of course, employed deliberately by Communists, Socialists and other revolutionaries. Unfortunately, it is also employed as a matter of thoughtless expediency by otherwise honest and dedicated persons, some at the highest levels of American leadership, who want social change so urgently that they act as if they believed their idealistic goals justified any means they can get away with.

THE CAUSE AND THE PARTY LINE

Please note that *the Cause* as used in this brief dictionary does not necessarily mean the cause of Communism, although this may be the case. It depends on the context within which the term is used. For example, it may also refer to the aspirations and activities of any militant group, such as the Black Panthers or the Students for a Democratic Society, which advocates and utilizes the illegal means of revolution to attain its particular objectives.

Similarly, the *Party Line* may describe the instructions to their followers issued by the Soviet, Red Chinese, or other Communist power center. Then again it may refer to the instructions of the leaders of revolutionary organizations whose aspirations and objectives, whether by design or by coincidence, promote the spread of Communism-Socialism, Hence the terms must be interpreted within the context in which they are used.

SOURCES OF MAIN ENTRIES

The Socialist/Communese terms defined in this Glossary include those frequently encountered by people who read the daily newspaper and listen to the news on radio and TV. The principal sources of the dictionary entries are the author's book on Communist semantics, *Conquest With Words* (Crestwood Books, Arlington, Va. 22202, 1967); his translation from Communese-English to standard English of *The Plans of the Communist Party of South Vietnam*, circulated in the United Nations in December 1967 as "The Political Programme of the National Liberation Front of South Vietnam"; other documents and statements prepared by Communists or revolutionaries; and words and phrases appearing in the press and heard on news broadcasts, particularly those dealing with the wars in Southeast Asia and the Middle East, to civil disorders in the streets and on college campuses, and to the attitudes and activities of pressure groups that "go outside the system" to accomplish their aims and fulfill their aspirations.

LIMITED NUMBER OF ENTRIES

It was neither necessary nor practical to define or translate the thousands of concepts found in English language dictionaries, although technically this is possible. It is believed the number and nature of the entries selected for inclusion in this brief Socialist/Communese Dictionary will satisfy some of the needs of the average person desiring to understand the international language of revolution—once he has grasped the logic behind its use.

GENERAL FORMAT

The Socialist/Communese main entries generally consist of concepts, although some slogans and other expressions have been listed. They have been printed alphabetically in bold type. Immediately following is their meaning in standard English. Whenever a Communist term is used in defining another Communist term, it is *italicized.* Dictionary meanings should be assigned to other words used in the definitions.

TRANSLATING WITH THIS DICTIONARY

Bold type is used for the purpose of distinguishing Social-ist/Communese words from standard English words. When-ever a word is printed in bold type, it should be interpreted in its ideological sense, and not in its normal sense.

It is hoped that dictionary users will readily grasp the principles which make Socialist/Communese a reliable and understandable language in its own right, so that they may learn how to make valid translations into everday speech without recourse to a dictionary.

The principles are simple: Whatever promotes *the Cause* or the *Party Line* is good, right and true. Whatever does not is bad, wrong and false. The Soviet Union and other Com-munist entities are good and should be supported; the United States and all phases of Capitalism are bad and should be destroyed. These are the bases for determining truth and falsity in Socialist/Communese.

300 EXAMPLES

ABSURD — Opposed to Marxist-Leninist logic; opposed to the Soviet or Com-munist viewpoint. Syn. *incorrect*. Ant. *correct*.

ACHIEVE JOINT ACTION WITH — To force or dupe into cooperation.

AGENT — n. A U.S. ally, e.g., The puppet government in South Vietnam is the *agent* of U.S. *imperialism*.

ACADEMIC FREEDOM — The freedom of professors and students to promote, by whatever means necessary, inside and outside of classrooms, the leftwing viewpoint on college campuses. Ant. *repression*.

ACCOMMODATION — Political concessions made by the U.S. to the Soviet Union.

ACTIVISTS — Professional Communist agitators, *student revolutionaries* or *stu-dent militants* trained as leaders, teachers, orators, propagandists, mob-inciters, experts in sabotage, espionage and terrorism, and specialists in handling uncon-ventional arms such as Molotov cocktails and acid bombs, who engage in activi-ties leading to the weakening or destruction of *The Establishment*.

AGITATION — Communist subversion which may be and usually is accompanied by or results in violence.

AGGRESSION — Defensive measures against Soviet or Communist aggression; armed resistance to a Communist takeover; national defense; resistance; opposi-tion. Ant. *liberation*.

AGREEMENT — Embodiment in writing of reciprocal promises between the pro-Communist or Communist side and the non-Communist side, to be kept by the former so long as politically expedient.

ANTI — Prefix. Opposed to the Socialist, collectivist, pro-Communist, Communist or Soviet position.

ANTI-COLONIALISM — The Soviet or Communist policy or practice of subverting undeveloped countries. Ant. *colonialism*, practiced only by non-Communist states, esp. the U.S.

ANTI-COMMUNIST — The policy, practice, or advocacy of democracy, capitalism and patriotism in preference to socialism, collectivism and *internationalism*.

ANTI-FACIST — One who fights against *anti-Communism*.

ANTI-IMPERIALISM — Anti-U.S.

ANTI-PEACE — adj. Opposed to the *Marxist-Leninist* version(s) of peace; opposed to Communist subversion and aggression; anti-Soviet; anti-Communist. Syn. *warmongering*; Ant. *peace-loving; anti-war.*

ANTI-WAR — Opposed to the U.S. or non-Communist side in a war; against resisting Communist aggression. Syn. *peace-loving*. Ant. *warmongering; anti-peace.*

ANTI-WAR DEMONSTRATION, MARCH, PETITION, RALLY, etc. — One that promotes opposition to the non-Communist participation in a war.

APATHETIC — Not interested in radical social change. Said of college students who merely want to get an education and show no inclination toward revolutionary activities.

ARMED SELF-DEFENSE — Armed offense against the law enforcement authorities and the government of the U.S. or other non-Communist country.

ARMS AGREEMENT — An international agreement which strengthens the Soviet or Communist side; a U.S. — Soviet agreement to reduce U.S. defensive capabilities, in effect, unilaterally. See *agreement*.

ATROCITIES — The inevitable, unintentional civilian casualties caused by armed resistance to Communist aggression.

AUNT JEMIMAS — Black women who advocate democratic and legal means for the redress of grievances. See *Uncle Toms*.

AUTHORITARIAN — Opposing, or lacking sympathy for, radicalism, Marxism, Socialism and Communism of the part of *The Establishment; intolerant of* violence and collectivist activities.

BAD — Bad for the Soviet Union or Communism in general. The quality of badness is always present in that which opposes the current *Party Line*. Ant. *good.*

BAN THE BOMB! — Slogan meaning: "Never consider using weapons against the Soviet Union under any circumstances!"

BLACK — adj. Of or pertaining to promoting revolutionary goals, for whatever reason, on the part of Negroes.

BLACK MILITANT — A Negro who advocates and practices violence in promoting revolutionary goals.

BLACK POWER — The policy and practice of using real or alleged racial injustice to justify lawless acts and unreasonable demands on the government or white community; the union of *black militants* and subversives, with whatever support they can muster, for the purpose of promoting revolutionary goals.

BOURGEOIS — adj. Of or pertaining to private property, the middle class in Western society, or the Western way of life. Often preceded by the adjective "petty" to intensify the contempt felt by those who use the word. By extension, non-Communist, anti-Communist, or Western; enemy. Syn. *middle class*. Ant. *Socialist, proletarian; people's.*

BOURGEOIS DEMOCRACY, GOVERNMENT, MENTALITY, etc. — Western democracy, government, mentality, morality, etc., contrasted with the Marxist-Leninist version of these concepts.

BOURGEOIS MORALITY — Western morality, the traditional ethical system of mankind, based on Natural Law. Ant. *New Morality*.

BRUTALITY — The use of physical restraint of any kind to cope with revolutionary activities. See *police brutality*.

BUILD — To make progress toward Socialism-Communist. Syn. *change*.

CAPITALISM — The free enterprise system, always held to be exploitative and oppressive in character, regardless of the facts; democracy; Western civilization; the enemy to be destroyed. adj. *capitalist, capitalistic*.

CAPITALIST — n. An exploiter; an oppressor.

CAUSE, THE — The Communist struggle for world domination; world revolution; any Soviet or Communist objective; the *Party Line*. Syn. *class struggle*.

CEASE-FIRE — An agreement providing for the cessation of hostilities and military build-up by the non-Communist side. See *agreement*.

CHANGE — To destroy or radically alter some democratic institution. Syn. *build*.

CHANGE THE UNIVERSITIES! — Destroy the universities!

CHAUVINISM — Patriotism; the love of one's native land in preference to the U.S.S.R. Ant. *international-mindedness*.

CIVIL DISOBEDIENCE — The theory and practice of a citizen's deciding for himself which laws to break in obedience to the *Party Line*. Ant. *law and order*.

CIVIL RIGHTS — Claims with an allegedly legal basis to justify illegal acts in pursuance of the *Party Line*.

CLASS CONSCIOUSNESS — The willingness to foment discord and disunity between classes and minority groups in pursuance of the *Party Line*.

CLASSLESS SOCIETY — The impossible Utopian dream promoted by Marxists and used as bait to attract pseudo-liberal support for Communist goals.

CLASS STRUGGLE — 1. The worldwide Communist strategy to divide classes and minority groups in capitalist countries in order to overthrow the government. — 2. The Communist struggle for world domination, currently consisting of two major tactics, following varying interpretations of Lenin's writings (Marxism-Leninism): a) The use of force, violence, or direct aggression primarily (*wars of liberation*) advocated by the Red Chinese power center, and b) The use of subversion, diplomacy, or indirect aggression (*peaceful coexistence*) advocated by the Soviet power center.

COALITION GOVERNMENT — The coexistence of Communist and non-Communist factions within a government, lasting until the Communists can maneuver themselves into complete control; the prelude to a Communist takeover.

COEXISTENCE — The temporary tolerance by Communists of non-Communists until they gain enough strength to destroy the non-Communists. See *peaceful coexistence*.

COLD WAR — An *international political climate* manipulated by the Kremlin involving undisguised hostility to the U.S., lack of cooperation, and threats of war. Ant. *peaceful coexistence*.

COLONIALISM — U.S. aid to, or Western influences in, an undeveloped nation; the dispatch of U.S. troops to a country threatened with a Communist takeover; possessing territory the Reds want. Ant. *Anti-colonialism*.

COLONIAL POWERS — Powerful non-Communist states, particularly the United States.

COLONY — A sovereign state receiving U.S. economic or military assistance to combat Communist aggression.

COMMON — Soviet or Communist. e.g. — The Soviet invasion and conquest of Czechoslovakia in 1968 was for the *common* good.

COMMON DEFENSE — Soviet or Communist defense.

COMMON INTERESTS — Soviet or Communist interests.

COMMON SENSE — Willingness to follow the *Party Line*, or accept the Soviet or Communist viewpoint. Syn. *reason; reasonableness*. Ant. *stubbornness*.

COMMUNICATE — To get one's viewpoint accepted.

COMMUNISM — A totalitarian, collectivistic way of life imposed by the Communist Party in the name of freedom and equality, portrayed as a respectable political philosophy. adj. *Communist*, Syn. *Socialism*. See *Marxism* and *Marxism-Leninism*. Ant. *Fascism*.

COMMUNITY — A group of people acting together in pursuance of the *Party Line*, or the area of their activities.

COMMUNITY ACTION — Group action by citizens in harmony with the *Party Line*.

COMPROMISE — An agreement reached by yielding to radical, revolutionary or Communist demands. See *agreement*.

CONFRONTATION — A deliberate defying of constituted authority by radical or subversive groups, with their followers, to provoke violence which is blamed on the restraining authority.

CONSERVATIVES — Those persons who espouse Capitalism and oppose Socialism-Communism. Ant. *liberals*.

CONSTITUTIONAL RIGHTS — Claims allegedly based on the U.S. Constitution to justify illegal acts in pursuance of the *Party Line*.

CONTROVERSIAL — 1. In reference to persons, groups, ideas, issues, etc. contrary to the *Party Line* — reprehensible. 2. In reference to those promoting the *Party Line* — praiseworthy.

COOPERATION — The act of working together for the benefit of Socialism-Communism.

CORRECT — adj. Conforming to the *Party Line*. Ant. *incorrect*.

CORRUPT — adj. Of or pertaining to any phase of Capitalism.

COUNTERREVOLUTIONARY — adj. In opposition to a Communist revolution. Syn. *reactionary*. Ant. *progressive*.

CREDIBILITY GAP — Disbelief and mistrust in official statements contrary to the *Party Line*, created by leftwing and communist propaganda.

CRIME — The action of authorities to curb illegal activities carried out in pursuance of the *Party Line*.

CRIMINAL DISCRIMINATION — Insistence that the civil rights of racial minorities shall be achieved through the operation of the democratic process and without violence or lawbreaking. See *law and order; police brutality; racism*.

CULTURAL ACTIVITIES — Those that promote the *Party Line*. Ant. *rightwing propaganda*.

CULTURE — Training and development in the Socialist-Communist mentality, morals and methods.

DE-ESCALATION — The unilateral, *justified* and *praiseworthy* reduction of military operations against Communist aggression. Ant. *escalation*.

DEMANDS — Irrational and often illegal requests, sometimes impossible of fulfillment, made on *The Establishment* by *militants* and *revolutionaries* in furtherance of *the Cause. Demands* are frequently nonnegotiable and accompanied by violence or threats of violence.

DEMOCRACY — A communist-type democracy; a collectivistic dictatorship; a totalitarian state controlled by the Communist Party elite. Syn. *Socialism; Communism; people's democracy.* Ant. *Facism; bourgeois democracy.*

DEMOCRATIC — Of or pertaining to the Marxist-Leninist version of democracy; Soviet or pro-Soviet; Communist or pro-Communist. The word is used to describe persons, organizations or policies which further Communist aims. See *democracy.* Syn. *Socialist.* Ant. *Fascist.*

DEMONSTRATION — A Party-Lining meeting, procession, or activity which frequently ends in civil disorders.

DENIAL OF RIGHTS — The refusal of *The Establishment* to give in to illegal or irrational demands and threats of violence.

DICTATORSHIP — Any anti-Communist government. Syn. *Fascism.* Ant. *(People's) Democratic. Republic; (Soviet) Socialist Republic; Socialism; Communism.*

DIRTY WAR — One in which the non-Communist side inflicts heavy casualties on the Communist side; hence, the Vietnam war.

DISARMAMENT — The unilateral disarmament of the United States in the hope the U. S. S. R. will follow suit. See *arms agreement.*

DISCRIMINATION — The advocacy of rational, legal and democratic policies and practices to achieve racial justice. See *criminal discrimination.* Syn. *racism.*

DISENFRANCHISEMENT OF THE AMERICAN PEOPLE — The rejection of radical, leftwing proposals, as at a national political convention. See *people.*

DISLOYALTY — Failure to carry out the *Party Line;* patriotic activities. Syn. *bourgeois loyalty.* Ant. *loyalty; proletarian loyalty.*

DISSENT — The use of violence and other illegal methods by a Party-Lining minority to express disagreement with the majority. Syn. *free speech; academic freedom.* Ant. *repression; denial of free speech, or academic freedom and civil, constitutional or human rights.*

DOVE — One who supports Communist war policy, especially in S.E. Asia. Syn. *peacelover.* Ant. *hawk; warmonger.*

EDUCATIONAL REFORM — Making students more receptive to Socialism and Communism.

ENLIGHTENED — Of or pertaining to the realization that Socialism-Communism is good and that the U.S. is the real enemy of mankind. Syn. *progressive.* Ant. *reactionary.*

EQUALITY — The state or quality of being advantageous to *The Cause.* Syn. *proletarian equality.* Ant. *bourgeois equality.*

ESCALATION — Unilateral, *unjustified* and *reprehensible* increase in military defense against Communist aggression. Ant. *de-escalation.*

ESTABLISHMENT, THE — Any kind of authority which hinders Communist objectives; the democratic system; the enemy; part of *the System.* Syn. *the power structure.*

EXERCISE RIGHTS (or FREEDOMS) — To use any possible means to promote Socialism-Communism.

EXPLOITATION — Reasonably fair and just treatment, as between employer and employee.

EXTRA-LEGAL MEANS — Subversion, rioting, assassination, blackmail, terrorism, etc. in pursuance of the *Party Line.* Ant. *legal means.*

EXTREMIST — One who advocates policies and practices in opposition to the *Party Line*.

FAIRNESS — Partiality to those persons or activities promoting the *Party Line*. Ant. *unfairness*.

FAIR SHARE — The Socialistic notion that those citizens who can't, don't, and/or won't work are rightfully entitled to financial support from those who can, do and/or will, the monies to be disbursed to the non-workers preferably by the Federal government from taxes collected from the workers.

FASCISM — Anti-Communism. Ant. *democracy*.

FASCIST — An active anti-Communist. Syn. *Nazi*.

FASCIST STATE — Any state, or any level of authority within that state, that forcibly restrains Communist activity.

FAVORABLE POLITICAL CLIMATE — The conditions in any area or country in which Socialism-Communism can flourish with relative impunity and without detection, usually during a period of *peaceful coexistence*. Ant. *unfavorable political climate*. See *political climate*.

FREE — 1. Outside the Communist world: having unlimited civil, political, or religious liberty in pursuance of the *Party Line*; lawless; anarchical; unrestrained; unrestricted. Ant. *oppressed; repressed*. 2. Inside the Communist world: having such civil, political or religious liberty as permitted by the ruling clique. Ant. *anti-Party; anti-Socialist; anti-Soviet*. n. *freedom*.

FREEDOM-LOVING — Favoring the Communist versions of freedom. See *free*. Ant. *warmongering*.

FREE SPEECH — License to promote the destruction of our free society.

FREE UNIVERSITY — A center, usually located on a college campus, featuring revolutionary courses and leftwing instructors dispensing anti-U.S. and pro-Socialist-Communist philosophies *Free universities* are frequently accorded physical facilities and encouraged by unsuspecting college administrations.

GENERATION GAP — The normal disagreement between parents and children regarding ethics and values, exploited and exacerbated by promotion of the *New Morality*, aided and abetted by pseudo-liberal professors, teachers, clergymen, writers and members of the news media, in deliberate or unwitting pursuance of the *Party Line*.

GENOCIDE — The systematic rout of Communist troops in battle; a series of non-Communist victories.

GESTAPO TACTICS — Forceful restraint of criminal Communist activities by law enforcement agencies in any non-Communist state.

GOOD — Good for the Soviet Union or Communism in general. The quality of goodness is always present in that which promotes the current *Party Line*. Ant. *bad*.

HARASSMENT — Diligent efforts by law enforcement officers to prevent illegal or subversive activities. If force is used, *police brutality* is normally charged.

HATE LITERATURE — Publications which identify and expose Communist strategy and tactics.

HAWK — One who opposes Communist war policy, especially in S.E. Asia. Ant. *dove*.

HITLERITE — Any anti-Communist. Syn. *Nazi; fascist*.

HUMAN RIGHTS — Any plausible rights that can be exploited to advance Socialism-Communism.

HUMANE TREATMENT — Ruthless exploitation for political advantage of prisoners of war, or of other persons in the power of the Soviets or Communists, including citizens of the U. S. S. R. and other Communist-ruled states.

HUMANISM — The character or quality of being human in accordance with standards set by the controlling Communist Party.

HUMANITARIANISM — The doctrine which advocates the expendability of the individual for the good of the Communist Party. Ant. *bourgeois* humanitarianism.

ILLEGAL — Contrary to the Marxist-Leninist representation of law, which holds that any act or condition that hurts Communism is *ipso facto* illegal. Ant. *legal*.

ILLEGAL WAR — A war against Soviet or Communist aggression, e.g., the U.S. defense of South Vietnam; non-Communist participation in such a war. Ant. *legal war*.

IMMORAL — Contrary to the Marxist-Leninist representation of morality, which holds that any act or condition that hurts Communism is *ipso facto* immoral. Ant. *moral*.

IMMORAL WAR — A war against Soviet or Communist aggression, e.g., the U.S. defense of South Vietnam; non-Communist participation in such a war. Ant. *moral war*.

IMPERIALISM — 1. U.S. policies and practices; 2. U.S. military opposition to Soviet or Communist aggression. Syn. 1. *Fascism*. 2. *aggression*. Ant. 1. *Socialism*. 2. *liberation*.

IMPERIALIST — n. An active anti-Communist. Syn. *Fascist; Hitlerite; Nazi; warmonger*. Ant. *Socialist; freedom-lover; peace-lover*.

INCORRECT — adj. Not conforming to the *Party Line*. Ant. *correct*.

INDEPENDENCE — The state or quality of being free from Western or capitalist influences, and being dependent on, and subservient to, the Soviet Union, or any other Communist power center. Syn. *freedom*. Ant. *bourgeois independence*.

INDEPENDENCE MOVEMENT — Communist aggression; an attempted Soviet or Communist takeover. Syn. *war of independence; liberation movement; war of (national) liberation*. Ant. *aggression, illegal, immoral, unjust, dirty, etc. war*.

INJUSTICE — Conformity with Western standards of justice. Syn. *bourgeois justice*. Ant. *justice*.

INQUISITION — The trial of any *militant* or *revolutionary* accused of criminal activities in pursuance of the *Party Line*.

INTERNATIONAL COOPERATION — Cooperation among nations and people for Soviet or Communist benefit. See *cooperation*.

INTERNATIONALISM — Mutual understanding and cooperation among nations and people to advance the Soviet or Communist welfare. Syn. *patriotism*. Ant. *chauvinism*.

INTERNATIONAL-MINDEDNESS — Patriotic feelings directed toward the Soviet Union rather than toward one's native land. Syn. *patriotism*. Ant. *chauvinism*.

INTERNATIONAL POLITICAL CLIMATE — The attitude of the non-Communist world, particularly the United States, toward the Soviet Union and Communism in general. Kremlin political warfare strategists recognize and manipulate two major types of political climates, the *Cold War* (threats of war) and *peaceful coexistence* (the seeming promise of peace). See *peaceful, coexistence, peaceful coexistence* and *Cold War.*

INTERNATIONAL TENSIONS — Strained East-West relations held to be caused by U.S. refusal to yield to Soviet demands. When the U.S. yields, tensions are said to be *reduced, lessened* or *eased.* When the U.S. does not yield, tensions are said to be *increased.*

INTIMIDATION — Any suggestion by an influential leader that the pseudo-liberal or Socialist-Communist viewpoint may be wrong and unfair.

INTOLERANCE — Opposition to, or lack of sympathy for, radicalism, Marxism, Socialism, Communism, the New Morality, etc. Ant. *tolerance.*

INVOLVEMENT — 1. In reference to activities promoting the *Party Line*: commendable and praiseworthy participation, to be encouraged. 2. In reference to activities detrimental to the *Party Line*: reprehensible and blameworthy participation, to be discouraged.

IRRELEVANT — Not fitting nor suiting requirements of the *Party Line.* Ant. *relevant.*

JUST — According to the Marxist-Leninist representation of justice, which holds that any act or condition that promotes Communism is *ipso facto* just. Ant. *unjust.*

JUSTICE — Conformity with the Socialist-Communist representation of justice. Syn. *proletarian justice.* Ant. *injustice; bourgeois justice.*

JUSTIFIED — Promoted some Socialist-Communist goal. Ant. *unjustified.*

JUST WAR — A war of Soviet or Communist aggression; the Soviet or Communist participation in such a war. Ant. *unjust war.*

KIDS — Young, idealistic pseudo-liberals, misguided by leftwing philosophies, bent on destruction of the American system by force, violence, and terrorism. Syn. *revolutionaries.*

LACKEY — One who supports U.S. foreign and domestic policy in opposition to the *Party Line.*

LAW AND ORDER — The alleged policy or practice of law enforcement authorities to use excessive force against the perpetrators of criminal acts in pursuance of the *Party Line.* See *police brutality.*

LEGAL — In conformity with the Marxist-Leninist representation of legality which holds that any act or condition that promotes Communism is *ipso facto* legal. Ant. *illegal.*

LEGAL LYNCHING — An impartial trial for a *black militant* accused of some crime.

LEGAL MEANS — Keeping within the law to promote the *Party Line.*

LEGAL WAR — Any Communist war of aggression. Ant. *illegal war.*

LESSEN INTERNATIONAL TENSIONS — To give in to Soviet or Communist demands. Ant. *increase international tensions.* See *international tensions.*

LIBERALS — Those persons who deliberately or unwittingly promote Socialism-Communism. Ant. *conservatives.*

LIBERATION — The act of freeing from traditional, Western or capitalist influences; the Communist takeover of a free country. Syn. *salvation.* Ant. *aggression, imperialism; reaction.*

LIBERATION FRONT — A subversive, Communist-dominated political organization, purporting to represent the people, which spearheads an attempted Communist takeover.

LIBERATION MOVEMENT — Any movement to destroy or weaken any phase of Capitalism; an attempted Communist takeover.

LOVE — 1. Sexual license promoted by the *Party Line* to weaken Western morals, at the same time causing abhorrence of war. 2. Love for Socialism-Communism and the Soviet Union above all else.

LOYALTY — Promotion of the *Party Line*; subversive activities. Syn. *bourgeois disloyalty*. Ant. *disloyalty*.

MAKE LOVE, NOT WAR! — Get your mind on sex and off Communist aggression.

MALE CHAUVINISM — The act or advocacy of the opposition of men, for whatever reason, to the *liberation* of women. Syn. *sexism*.

MARXISM — Idealistic, impractical, theoretical Communism.

MARXISM-LENINISM — Practical Communism; a system of world enslavement under the Russian Communist Party elite; precepts to bring about world Communism, based on the principles of ideological expediency advanced by Lenin.

McCARTHYISM — Any action to expose Communist espionage and subversion; anti-Communism.

MEANINGFUL DIALOGUE — A discussion between members of the radical left and the authorities, resulting in the latter acceding to the *demands* of the former.

MIDDLE CLASS CULTURE, MENTALITY, MORALITY, etc. — Western culture, mentality, morality, etc., contrasted with the Marxist-Leninist version of these concepts.

MILITANT — One who advocates or uses force, violence, and terrorism to carry out the *Party Line*.

MILITARISM — The policy and practice of maintaining adequate defense against Communist aggression; national defense.

MILITARISTS — Western leaders, especially American, who advocate adequate national defense. Syn. *warmongers*. Ant. *peacelovers*.

MILITARY-INDUSTRIAL COMPLEX — The heart and guts of the American defense against Communist aggression.

MOBILIZATION — The marshalling of support for some goal of Socialism-Communism.

MODERATES — Those who see little danger in Socialism-Communism, especially the Soviet brand. Ant. *extremists; rightwingers*.

MORAL — In conformity with the Marxist-Leninist representation of morality, which holds that any act or condition that promotes Communism is *ipso facto* moral. Ant. *immoral*.

MORAL WAR — Communist aggression; the Communist participation in a war against non-Communists. Ant. *immoral war*.

MUTUAL ASSISTANCE — Non-Communist help for the Communists.

MUTUAL CONCESSIONS — Concessions by both sides regarding the manner of yielding to Soviet or Communist demands.

MUTUAL COOPERATION — Cooperation for Soviet or Communist benefit.

MUTUAL TRUST — Reliance on Soviet or Communist promises.

MYTH — Facts at variance with the current *Party Line*, particularly as regards Soviet foreign policy interpretation. Ant. *political realities*.

NAZI — Any anti-Communist. Syn. *Hitlerite; fascist*.

NEGOTIATIONS — A means to win concessions from the non-Communist side.

NEO-COLONIALISM — U.S. support against Communist aggression at the request of another sovereign state.

NEUTRALITY — Bias toward Communism.

NEUTRAL NATION — An ostensibly neutral nation pressured into promoting the Communist cause.

NEW — Favorable to *The Cause*. Ant. *decadent*.

NEW LEFT — A loosely-knit consortium of leftwingers bent on destroying the United States government by any means that they can get away with.

NEW MORALITY — An ethical system based on an individual's personal determination of right and wrong, an outgrowth of permissivism and situation ethics; the old immorality. Ant. *bourgeois morality; middle class* morals.

NONAGGRESSION TREATY — An East-West, or Soviet-satellite treaty, stipulating that under no circumstances will the non-Communist, or non-Soviet, signatories attack the Communist signatories, or the Soviet signatory. See *treaty*.

NONVIOLENT MEANS — Inciting a peaceful protest gathering to violence and blaming it on police brutality. See *violent means*.

NORMAL — Favorable to the Soviet Union or Communism.

NORMALIZE — To establish, or re-establish, comprehensive Soviet or Communist control.

NORMAL RELATIONS — Relations favorable to the Soviet or Communist side.

OPPRESSED MINORITIES — Any minorities in a non-Communist country.

OPPRESSED PEOPLE — Those not living under Communism.

OPPRESSION — The alleged state or condition of people not living under Communism.

OVERKILL — U.S. military capacity or national defense equal to, or superior to, the Soviet Union's.

OVERREACTION — Using sufficient means, especially force, to cope successfully with illegal activity carried out in pursuance of the *Party Line*. Syn. *police brutality*.

PARTICIPATORY DEMOCRACY — Participation in protests, demonstrations, marches, riots, terrorism, guerrilla warfare, etc., in pursuance of the *Party Line*; violent group reaction to any form of authority; mob rule. Syn. *liberation*.

PARTY LINE — Instructions from the Soviet Union, to be obeyed without questioning by Communists of all nationalities. Since the Sino-Soviet ideological split, the Red Chinese Communist Party also has a *Party Line*, which frequently conflicts with the Soviet instructions.

PATRIOTISM — Allegiance to the Soviet Union, regardless of one's citizenship; obedience to the *Party Line*. Syn. *Internationalism*. Ant. *chauvinism; treason*.

PEACE — 1. Absence or cessation of resistance to Communist aggression; hence. a Communist victory. 2. Western policy or practice favorable to promotion of the *Party Line*. 3. An international climate in which Communism can flourish. Ant. *aggression; war, unjust, immoral, illegal*, etc., *wars; warmongering policies or practices*.

PEACE CANDIDATE — A candidate for public office who advocates foreign policy which would, in effect, aid a Communist victory.

PEACE DEMONSTRATION, MARCH, PETITION, RALLY, etc. — Mass gatherings or activities to promote any of the Communist brands of peace. Syn. *anti-war demonstration*, etc.

PEACEFUL — Not resisting promotion of the *Party Line*, or Communist aggression; unresisting. Ant. *warmongering*.

PEACEFUL ASSEMBLY — Any gathering of people to be manipulated to carry out the *Party Line*, whether legally and peacefully, or illegally and violently.

PEACEFUL COEXISTENCE — 1. The temporary toleration of the existence of the non-Communist faction, side, state, etc., ending when the Communist coexisters gain sufficient strength to liquidate the non-Communists; hence, a breathing space for the Communist side. 2. A means to obtain the unwitting assistance of the U.S. in bringing about its own downfall in a seemingly peaceful world climate; hence, nonresistance to Soviet indirect aggression.

PEACEFUL SETTLEMENT or SOLUTION — One that advances the Communist cause.

PEACELOVER — One who promotes any of the Communist brands of peace. Ant. *warmonger*.

PEOPLE — n. 1. Communists or collectivists. 2. Supporters of the *Party Line* for whatever reason. 3. The Communist Party. 4. A Communist state. 5. The Party elite, or those who control Party policy. adj. *popular; people's*. Syn. *proletariat; masses; populace; population; working class; progressives*. Ant. *Facists; Nazis; reactionaries; imperialists; warmongers*.

PEOPLE'S DEMOCRACY or DEMOCRATIC REPUBLIC — A collectivistic, authoritarian system of government, dependent on and subservient to the Soviet Union, Red China, or other Communist power center.

PERSECUTION — The legal prevention of illegal acts committed in pursuance of the *Party Line*.

PIETY — Fervor for a social revolution among church leaders.

PIG — A law enforcement officer, especially when preventing acts of violence committed in pursuance of the *Party Line*.

POLARIZATION — The act of, or the effect from, exposing pseudo-liberal bias, superficialities and inconsistencies with vigor and clarity. Ant. *solidarity*.

POLICE BRUTALITY — The policy or practice of law enforcement officers to use force in opposition to the *Party Line*. Syn. *law and order; police state tactics; overreaction*.

POLICE HARASSMENT — Enforcement of the law against leftwing and revolutionary criminals.

POLICE STATE — One that vigorously restrains criminal Communist activities.

POLITICAL ACTIVITIES or WORK — Communist indoctrination or subversion.

POLITICAL PRISONER — A Communist or leftwinger caught committing a crime.

POPULAR — Communist, Communist-oriented, Communist-controlled, Communist-backed, or pro-Communist. Syn. *people's*.

POWER STRUCTURE, THE — Any form of organized authority in a non-Communist state; the enemy; part of *the System*. Syn. *the Establishment*.

POWER TO THE PEOPLE! — Power to the Communists! See *people*.

PRAISEWORTHY — Deserving praise for helping *the Cause*. Ant. *reprehensible*.

PRISONER OF WAR — Any non-Communist who happens to fall into the hands of guerrillas, revolutionaries or Communists.

PROGRESSIVE — adj. Promoting the *Party Line*. n. One who promotes the *Party Line*. Ant. *reactionary*.

PROLETARIAN — adj. Communist; the Marxist-Leninist version of e.g., a *proletarian* democracy is democracy Communist-style, and *proletarian* international law is the Marxist-Leninist version of international law. n. *proletariat*.

PROPAGANDA — Views with which Communists disagree, especially those running contrary to the *Party Line* or Soviet foreign Policy.

PROTEST DEMONSTRATION, MARCH, MOVEMENT, etc. — Mass action to promote the *Party Line.*

PROVOCATION — Non-Communist response to illegal acts committed in pursuance of the *Party Line.* Ant. *self-defense; resistance, reprisal.*

PUBLIC OPINION — What people can be led to believe; the Communist version of events.

RACIAL DISCRIMINATION — Advocacy or practice of rational, democratic, and legal means to achieve racial justice. Same as *racism.*

RACISM — See *racial discrimination.* Syn. *law and order; police brutality; oppression.* Ant. *participatory democracy; liberation.*

REAL — The Communist version of, e.g., *real* independence is the Communist version of independence. See *independence.*

REACTIONARY — adj. In opposition to the *Party Line.* n. One who opposes the *Party Line.* Ant. *progressive.*

REALITY — The Communist version. Often used in the plural. Ant. *myth.*

REASON (or REASONABLENESS) — Willingness to follow the *Party Line,* or accept the Soviet or Communist viewpoint. Syn. *common sense.* Ant. *stubbornness.*

REASONABLE — Making good sense by Marxist Leninist standards. Syn. *correct.* Ant. *unreasonable.*

RELEVANT — Fitting or suiting requirements of the *Party Line.* Ant. *irrelevant.*

RELEVANT EDUCATION — Educational courses or methods the effect of which is to create discontent and foment revolution.

RELIGION — A vehicle for promoting the *Party Line* through pseudo-liberal religious leaders and groups.

RELIGIOUS BIGOT — One who opposes Communist inroads in religion.

RE-ORDER PRIORITIES — To make adjustments, as in the national budget, so as to allot more funds for socialistic activities at the expense of national defense.

REPREHENSIBLE — Deserving condemnation for hindering *the Cause.* Ant. *praiseworthy.*

REPRESSION — Restraints on illegal activities. Ant. exercise of civil, constitutional, human, etc., *rights.* v. *to repress.*

REPRISAL — Retaliation against *The Establishment* for enforcing the law, or against non-Communists for defending themselves against Communist aggression. Ant. *police brutality; aggression; provocation.*

RESISTANCE — Opposition to the restraints on illegal activities. Syn. *self-defense.*

RESISTANCE WAR (or WAR OF RESISTANCE) — Communist aggression.

RESTRUCTURE SOCIETY — To destroy society.

REVOLUTION — The elimination of all traces of Capitalism by any means possible.

REVOLUTIONARY — adj. Of or pertaining to the destruction of Capitalism. n. One dedicated to the destruction of Capitalism.

REVOLUTIONARY GOVERNMENT — The Communist government replacing an overthrown legitimate government.

RIGHT OF DISSENT — The Communist duty or obligation to take exception to all aspects of Western civilization, by any means feasible, in conformity with the *Party Line.*

RIGHT OF FREE SPEECH — The Communist duty or obligation to say or write, in conformity with the *Party Line*, anything whatsoever, at any time, under any circumstances, without regard for law, rule or regulation, custom, propriety and common decency, public safety, public morals, or the national interest and welfare.

RIGHT OF PEACEFUL ASSEMBLY — The allegation of a "right" by leftwingers and Communists to justify mob action in pursuance of the *Party Line*.

RIGHTS — Any means to promote the *Party Line*.

RIGHTWINGERS — Those who vigorously oppose Socialism-Communism. Ant. *moderates*.

SELF-DEFENSE — Armed resistance to restraints on illegal activities. Syn. *resistance*.

SELF-DETERMINATION — The right of a people to live under Communism.

SEXISM — The act or advocacy of opposition, for whatever reason, to the *liberation* of women. Syn. *male chauvinism*.

SOCIAL — Of or pertaining to collectivism, Socialism, or Communism; collectivistic; pro-Socialist; Communist-oriented.

SOCIAL ADJUSTMENT — Adjustment to collectivist methods and practices.

SOCIAL DEVELOPMENT — Development of collectivist methods and practices.

SOCIAL GOALS — Collectivist methods and practices leading to Socialism, and then Communism.

SOCIAL JUSTICE — The promotion of Socialism-Communism through legislation and court action.

SOCIALISM — 1. A state-controlled collectivistic society ripe for plucking by the Communists. 2. A euphemism for Communism. Adj. *socialist*.

SOCIAL REVOLUTION — An attempt to establish Socialism in a capitalist country.

SOCIAL SIGNIFICANCE — Having importance from the Socialist-Communist viewpoint.

SOCIAL STUDIES — High school and college courses depicting Socialism to be better than our present system of free enterprise, i.e., Capitalism.

SOLIDARITY — Cohesion and oneness of thought and action in carrying out the *Party Line*. Ant. *polarization*.

STATUS QUO — The expansion of Communism; the global struggle to destroy Capitalism; the Soviet march toward world domination; Communist imperialism. Syn. *The Cause; class struggle; liberation*. Atn. *aggression; repression; oppression*.

STOP THE WAR! — Stop the U.S. half of the war!

STUBBORNNESS — Refusal to follow the *Party Line*, or to accept the Soviet or Communist viewpoint. Ant. *common sense*.

STUDENT — A campus supporter of the *Party Line* for any reason. Usually used in the plural.

STUDENT POWER — The power of *students* to disrupt and destroy an educational institution.

SYSTEM, THE — The enemy democratic system to be attacked, weakened and destroyed, especially its sources of power. See *the Establishment* and *the power structure*.

TEACH-IN — Propagation of the *Party Line* in an academic atmosphere by means of "loaded" discussion panels and audience participation.

TOKENISM — Submission to, and compliance with radical, ultraleft demands; an integration effort of any magnitude.

TOLERANCE — Support or sympathy for radicalism, Marxism, Socialism, Communism, the New Morality, etc. Ant. *intolerance.*

TREASON — Disloyal acts toward the Soviet Union by citizens of any nationality, disobedience to, or deviation from, the *Party Line.* Ant. *patriotism; internationalism.*

TREATY — A Soviet-type or Communist-type international agreement made for the purpose of gaining strength. See *agreement.*

TRUCE — A Communist-type agreement providing for the cessation of hostilities and military build-up by the non-Communist side. See *agreement.*

TRUTH — Any thought or utterance which promotes the *Party Line.*

UNCLE TOMS — Black men who advocate democratic and legal means for the redress of grievances. See *Aunt Jemimas.*

UNFAIRNESS — Impartial treatment with respect to persons and activities promoting the *Party Line.* Ant. *fairness.*

UNFAVORABLE POLITICAL CLIMATE — Unfavorable conditions in any area or country for Socialism-Communism to flourish, frequently occurring during the *Cold War* period. Ant. *favorable political climate.* See *international political climate.*

UNJUST — According to the Marxist-Leninist representation of injustice, which holds that any act or condition that hinders Communism is *ipso facto* unjust. Ant. *just.*

UNJUSTIFIED — Hindered some Socialist-Communist goal. Ant. *justified.*

UNJUST WAR — A war against Soviet or Communist aggression; the U.S. or non-Communist participation in such a war. Ant. *just war.*

UNREASONABLE — Not conforming to the *Party Line.* Syn. *incorrect.* Ant. *reasonable.*

USURP THE POLITICAL PROCESS — To proceed in the traditional American way of nominating and electing public officials; to prevent *militants* and *revolutionaries* from destroying the political process.

VIETNAMIZATION — The strengthening of the South Vietnamese army to the point of its being able to repel Communist aggression without the help of U.S. ground troops. Hence, a "trick" to deprive the Vietnamese Communists of victory.

VIOLENT MEANS — The admitted use of violence in carrying out the *Party Line.* See *nonviolent means.*

VOLUNTEERS — Communist-controlled people coerced into carrying out the dictates of the Communist Party.

WAR — Armed resistance to Communist aggression, e.g., the Vietnam *War* and the *war* in the Middle East. The non-Communist participation in such a war. Syn. *aggression.* Ant. *peace; liberation.* See *anti-war, dirty war, illegal war, immoral war, just war, unjust war, war of (national) liberation,* and *STOP THE WAR!*

WAR CRIME — Any non-Communist military act which hampers the Communist war effort and has potential propaganda value.

WARMONGER — Anyone who advocates retaliation or defense against Soviet or Communist provocations, threats, or aggression. Syn. *hawk.* Ant. *peacelover; dove.* adj. *warmongering.* Ant. *peaceloving.*

WAR OF INDEPENDENCE — An attempted Communist takeover. Syn. *independence movement; war of (national) liberation.* Ant. *aggression.*
WAR OF (NATIONAL) LIBERATION — An attempted Communist takeover. Syn. *liberation movement; war of independence; independence movement.* Ant. *aggression.*
WE WANT PEACE! — We want a Communist victory! See *peace.*
WILL OF THE PEOPLE — The policies and practices of the Communist Party; the *Party Line.* (See *people*).
WOMEN'S LIBERATION MOVEMENT — "Women's Lib," a radical feminist movement ostensibly aimed at securing equality for women and manipulated by the New Left to weaken the U.S. social, political and social structure.
WORLD — adj. The Communist version of, e.g., *world* opinion is the Communist representation of events (see *public opinion*), and *world peace* is a *pax sovietica* (see *peace*).

PUBLICATIONS ON COMMUNIST SEMANTICS

For those wishing to explore further the important field of Communist semantics, three publications are especially recommended, in addition to *Conquest With Words*, previously mentioned. They are as follows:

(a) *Wordsmanship — Semantics as a Communist Weapon*, prepared for the Senate Internal Security Subcommittee by Dr. Stefan T. Possony, U.S. Government Printing Office, Washington, D.C., 1961.

(b) *Language as a Communist Weapon*, prepared in consultation with Dr. Stefan T. Possony by the House Committee on Un-American Activities, U.S. Government Printing Office, Washington, D.C., 1959.

(c) *Words in Sheep's Clothing*, Dr. Mario Pei, Hawthorn Books, N.Y., 1969.

PART III

APPENDIX

The following Foreword and the list of Speakers' Honoraria at Colleges and Universities under ORGANIZATIONAL ANALYSIS, is reproduced from the REPORT by the COMMITTEE ON INTERNAL SECURITY, HOUSE OF REPRESENTATIVES, Ninety-first Congress, second session.[*]

The Epilogue following the ORGANIZATIONAL ANALYSIS is reproduced from the same report.

[*] The full report is available for 30¢ from the Superintendent of Documents, U.S. Government Printing Office, Washington, D.C. 20402. Ask for House Report No. 91-1732.

The pictures on the back of this page and page 116 are not in the government report.

Police manned fences and kept spectators away from the University of Wisconsin (Madison) Math Research Center on August 25, 1970 while federal agents, aided by a tractor, search rubble for clues in the bombing of the building on August 24th. UPI

When the House Committee on Internal Security was established early in 1969, it was mandated by the House of Representatives to investigate "the extent, character, objectives, and activities within the United States" of any organizations or groups seeking to establish a dictatorship in this country or attempting to overthrow or alter our form of government by unlawful means. HCIS was further mandated to conduct similar investigations of organization or groups, their members and affiliates, which use violence or terrorism to obstruct the government so as to affect internal security.

During that first year of the Committee's life, we directed most of our attention to the radical Students for a Democratic Society which not only comprised the largest student movement ever to engulf the campuses of America's colleges and universities but which served as the handmaiden of revolutionary militancy and violence among the nation's youth.

By investigation, research and public hearings, HCIS published clear evidence that SDS was becoming increasingly dedicated to the principles of Marxism-Leninism and Maoism, employing the violent tactics of "the politics" of physical confrontation and establishing goals designed to destroy our system of government, its basic institutions, public property and—wherever possible or feasible—all manifestations of America's fundamentally democratic society.

By early 1970, though SDS was breaking apart into small factions engaged in varying degrees of militancy, at least a portion of its hard-core leadership channeled their energies and resources into acts of outright terrorism, punctuated by arson, bombing and attempted sabotage.

Other investigations by our Committee into (1) the organizers of so-called Mobilization demonstrations to end the way in Vietnam and into (2) the avowedly revolutionary paramilitary organization of the Black Panthers, produced ample evidence to show that these groups—like SDS—were being subverted to further the objectives of those wishing to tear down this nation and to deny Americans the right of domestic tranquillity.

Around the fringes of such organizations and, sometimes, at their very core, lurked the theoreticians and policy publicists of various communist organizations, the Communist Party USA, the Trotskyite Socialist Workers Party and the pro-Peking Progressive Labor Party.

Radicalization of students was advanced on many campuses by an assortment of speakers ranging from pseudo-intellectuals who exaggerated what may be bad about our society to anarchists and nihilists who denounced even that which is good about America. In far too many instances, such radical orators (by preaching disruption, destruction and violence) would appear to transcend the cherished First Amendment rights of free speech. The radicalizing effect of orators of SDS, Black Panther and other organizations was repeatedly demonstrated in Committee hearings. They addressed students whenever convenient, on a mall, in a dormitory or in classrooms. And for the privilege of often seeming to incite impressionable audiences to riotous behavior or resistance to law, such persons were reported as receiving as honoraria rather handsome fees.

The attorney who provided counsel for those found guilty of travelling interstate to start a riot during the 1968 Democratic National Convention in Chicago—Mr. William Kunstler—told newsmen after a speaking appearance at the University of Cincinnati in the spring of 1970:

"We raise most of the money for our movement through speaking engagements."

Similar claims have been made by others in that so-called "Chicago conspiracy" trial as well as by spokesmen for the Black Panthers. In early March of this year, FBI Director J. Edgar Hoover disclosed to the House Subcommittee on Appropriations:

"The sources of contributions to the Black Panther Party are many and varied . . . Black Panther leaders frequently fill speaking engagements at secondary schools, colleges and universities where they receive honorariums of up to $1,900 for each engagement as well as transportation costs. BPP speakers made 189 appearances at these educational institutions during the 1969 calendar year." For a number of years, Mr. Hoover has reported on the campus speaking engagements of members of the Communist Party, USA.

Since our Committee does have the authority to ascertain for the Congress the source of financing of revolutionary organizations and movements in the United States, I ordered the Committee research staff to conduct a preliminary survey of public source material regarding campus speaking appearances by radical extremists.

The report that resulted from this disclosed 120 instances of radical orators having addressed college and university student audiences. Frequent appearances were made by Jerry Rubin and Abbie Hoffman of the Youth International Party (YIPPIE) and other defendants in the "Chicago conspiracy" trial such as David Dellinger and Rennie Davis. Black Panther leader Eldridge Cleaver, though now in exile in exile in Algeria, made a number of appearances, as had Black Power advocate Stokely Carmichael. Both of these men have urged the destruction of the United States and called for a race war of revolution to further their goals. Another was H. "Rap" Brown who made campus speaking appearances prior to his disappearance on the eve of a Maryland trial for riot incitement.

Endeavoring to avoid raising any fears of interference with academic freedom or First Amendment rights, the Committee chose not to use the available power of subpoena. The Committee was persuaded, however, that the Congress had a right to know whether the amounts of honoraria paid such speakers was significant.

It was accordingly resolved that a canvass would be made of a proportion of American colleges, to seek their voluntary assistance in compiling data on speakers to ascertain whether honoraria might be a substantial source of revenue for the "revolutionary movement."

The survey, as described in this report, was then conducted and it is herewith presented to the House of Representatives by the Committee on Internal Security, pursuant to the rules of the House (particularly House Resolution 89 of the 91st Congress) which authorizes and directs the Committee to make reports of the results of investigations on the subjects of inquiry committed to it.

RICHARD H. ICHORD, *Chairman.*

ORGANIZATIONAL ANALYSIS
BLACK PANTHER PARTY (officer, member or supporter)

Name	Date	Source of funds	Honorarium
Elaine Brown	Feb. 19, 1970	Institutional funds	$100
H. Rap Brown	Dec. 8, 1969	Student funds	1,540
Don Cox	Oct. 2, 1969	Unknown	Unknown
Harry Edwards	Feb. 15, 1969	Student funds	1,100
Charles Garry	Apr. 13, 1970	do	250
Fred Hampton	Apr. 17, 1969	Collection	Unknown
Floyd Hardwick	Apr. 13, 1970	Unknown	200
Masai Hewitt	Feb. 16, 1970	Student funds	500
Paul Jacobs	Oct. 22, 1968	Institutional funds	200
	Feb. 14, 1969	Student funds	1,250
LeRoi Jones	Feb. 24, 1969	do	1,000
	Feb. 25, 1969	do	1,000
	Apr. 10, 1969	do	1,750
	Feb. 21, 1970	do	1,500
Robert Scheer	Sept. 24, 1969	Unknown	1,250
	Feb. 10, 1970	Student funds	1,200
	Feb. 12, 1970	Institutional funds	1,000
Bobby Seale	May 7, 1969	Collection	Unknown
Reies Tijerina	Sept. 24, 1968	Unknown	Unknown
	May 21, 1969	do	Unknown
	May 1969	Student funds	500

Note: Total number of speakers 13; total number of speeches 21; total known amount paid to speakers $14,340; average honorarium per speech where amount known $896.25.

CITED FOR CONTEMPT IN CONNECTION WITH "CHICAGO SEVEN" CONSPIRACY TRIAL [1]

Name	Date	Source of funds	Honorarium
Rennard Davis	Oct. 24, 1969	Student funds	$500.00
	April, 1970	Unknown	Unknown
David Dellinger	May 5, 1970	Student funds	1,224.00
	May 15, 1970	Collection	Unknown
John Froines	Feb. 8, 1970	Student funds	225.00
	May 15, 1970	Collection	Unknown
Tom Hayden	Dec. 3, 1968	Institutional funds	600.00
	Jan. 9, 1969	Student funds	300.00
	Feb. 14, 15, 1969	do	1,400.00
	Sept. 23, 1969	Collection	Unknown
	Jan. 17, 1970	Student funds	1,000.00
Abbie Hoffman	Apr. 22, 1969	Student funds	750.00
	Mar. 30, 1970	Unknown	119.70
	Apr. 11, 1970	Student funds	2,000.00
	Apr. 13, 1970	Unknown	1,300.00
	May 5, 1970	Student funds	1,224.00
William Kunstler	Nov. 14, 1969	Collection	Unknown
	Feb. 19, 1970	do	Unknown
	Feb. 25, 1970	Student funds	2,000.00
	Apr. 1, 1970	do	1,500.00
	Apr. 14, 1970	do	1,000.00
	May 12, 1970	do	1,500.00
Jerry Rubin	Jan. 7, 1969	Student funds	300.00
	Apr. 6, 1970	do	500.00
	Apr. 10, 1970	Collection	Unknown
	May 5, 1970	Student funds	1,224.00

[1] Lee Weiner (7th member of the conspiracy 7). No information in survey returns indicating this name.

Note: Total number of speakers 7; total number of speeches 26; total known amount paid to speakers $18,666.70; average honorarium per speech where amount known $982.46.

COMMUNIST PARTY OF THE UNITED STATES OF AMERICA

Name	Date	Source of funds	Honorarium
Herbert Aptheker	Apr. 10, 1969	Student funds	$600
	Nov. 17, 1969	Unknown	Unknown
Jesus Colon	Sept. 24, 1969	do	Unknown
Angela Davis	Nov. 4, 1969	Institutional funds	100
	Nov. 6, 1969	Student funds	200
Charles Garry	Apr. 13, 1969	do	250
Claude Lightfoot	Mar. 11, 1969	Unknown	Unknown
Charlene Mitchell	Oct. 9, 1969	do	Unknown
Jessica Mitford	Mar. 9, 1970	Institutional funds	676
Sidney Peck	Nov. 17, 1969	do	50
Michael Zagarell	Oct. 18, 1969	None	None

Note: Total number of speakers 9; total number of speeches 11; total known amount paid to speakers $1,876; average honorarium per speech where amount known $312.67.

NATION OF ISLAM

NAME	Date	Source of funds	Honorarium
Muhammad Ali	Feb. 2, 1969	Institutional funds	$500
	Mar. 5, 1969	Student funds	1,100
	Mar. 12, 1969	do	1,000
	Mar. 18, 1969	Institutional funds	1,000
	Apr. 8, 1969	Student funds	1,250
	May 26, 1969	Institutional funds	Unknown

Note: Total number of speakers 1; total number of speeches 6; total known amount paid to speakers $4,850; average honorarium per speech, where amount known $970.

NATIONAL MOBILIZATION COMMITTEE TO END THE WAR IN VIETNAM

(Officer, Member or Supporter)

Name	Date	Honorarium Source of funds	
James Bevel	Nov. 12, 1968	Institutional funds	$200
	do	do	100
Dick Gregory	Sept. 19, 1968	Student funds	1,250
	Oct. 21, 1968	do	1,000
	Nov. 6, 1968	do	1,250
	Dec. 12, 1968	do	1,250
	Jan. 7, 1969	do	1,000
	Feb. 18, 1969	do	500
	Feb. 25, 1969	Institutional funds	1,250
	Oct. 9, 1969	Unknown	Unknown
	Oct. 30, 1969	do	900
	Dec. 10, 1969	do	Unknown
	February 1970	Student funds	1,250
	Feb. 4, 1970	do	1,250
	Feb. 5, 1970	do	1,000
	Feb. 17, 1970	do	1,100
	Mar. 5, 1970	Unknown	Unknown
	Mar. 8, 1970	Student funds	750
	Mar. 10, 1970	Institutional funds	1,000
	Mar. 20, 1970	Student funds, ($500), institutional funds ($500).	1,000
	Apr. 9, 1970	Student funds	1,250
	Apr. 16, 1970	do	1,500
	July 23, 1970	Institutional funds	1,250
Edward Keating	Nov. 20, 1969	do	350

Note: Total number of speakers 3; total number of speeches 24; total known amount paid to speakers $20,400; average honorarium per speech where amount known $971.

NEW MOBILIZATION COMMITTEE TO END THE WAR IN VIETNAM
(officer, member or supporter)

Name	Date	Source of funds	Honorarium
David Dellinger	May 5, 1970	Student funds	$1,224
	May 15, 1970	Collection	Unknown
Douglas Dowd	May 7, 1970	None	None
Richard R. Fernandez	Nov. 15, 1969	Student funds	415
Carlton Goodlett	Oct. 1, 1968	Institutional funds	150
Stewart Meacham	Dec. 6, 1968	Student funds	70
Sidney Peck	Nov. 17, 1969	do	50
Mulford Q. Sibley	Jan. 28, 1969	do	100
Benjamin Spock	Oct. 1, 1968	do	1,000
	Oct. 31, 1968	do	2,250
	Apr. 16, 1969	do	1,500
	Sept. 24, 1969	do	2,000
	Sept. 25, 1969	do	2,000
	Oct. 3, 1969	Institutional funds	2,000
	Jan. 23, 1970	Student funds	1,750
	Feb. 14, 1970	do	2,500
	Apr. 3, 1970	do	1,100
	Apr. 16, 1970	do	2,000
	Apr. 18, 1970	do	1,750

Note: Total number of speakers 8; total number of speeches 19; total known amount paid to speakers $21,809; average honorarium per speech where amount known $1,282.88.

SOCIALIST WORKERS PARTY
(officer, member or supporter)

Name	Date	Source of Funds	Honorarium
Paul Boutelle	Oct. 9, 1969	Unknown	Unknown
	Nov. 20, 1969	Collection	Unknown
Nat Hentoff	Aug. 4, 1969	do	$1,250
	Oct. 13, 1969	do	1,250
	Oct. 22, 1969	Institutional funds	700
	Jan. 14, 1970	Student funds	1,500
Daniel Watts	July 16, 1968	Unknown	750
	Nov. 14, 1968	do	750
	Mar. 9, 1970	Student funds	750

Note: Total number of speakers 3; total number of speeches 9; total known amount paid to speakers $6,950; average honorarium per speech where amount known $993.

SPRING MOBILIZATION COMMITTEE TO END THE WAR IN VIETNAM
(officer, member or supporter)

Name	Date	Source of funds	Honorarium
Deirdre Griswold	Oct. 22, 1969	Unknown	Unknown
Nat Hentoff	Aug. 4, 1969	Student funds	$1,250
	Oct. 13, 1969	do	1,250
	Oct. 22, 1969	Institutional funds	700
	Jan. 14, 1970	Student funds	1,500
Staughton Lynd	Feb. 14, 1969	Student funds	900
	Oct. 15, 1969	Collection	Unknown
	Nov. 13, 1969	do	Unknown
Floyd McKissick	Mar. 17, 1969	Student funds	2,250
Jerome Skolnick	Nov. 21, 1969	do	350

Note: Total number of speakers 5; total number of speeches 10; total known amount paid to speakers $8,200; average honorarium per speech where amount known $1,171.43.

STUDENTS FOR A DEMOCRATIC SOCIETY (SDS)
(officer, member or supporter)

Name	Date	Source of funds	Honorarium
Robert Avakian	No date indicated	Unknown	Unknown
William Bunge	Apr. 24, 1969	Institutional funds	$150.00
Carl Davidson	September 1969	Unknown	Unknown
Rennard Davis	Oct. 24, 1969	Student funds	500.00
	April 1970	Unknown	Unknown
Tom Hayden	Dec. 3, 1968	Institutional funds	600.00
	Jan. 9, 1969	Student funds	300.00
	Feb. 14, 15, 1969	do	1,400.00
	Sept. 23, 1969	Unknown	Unknown
	Jan. 17, 1970	Student funds	1,000.00
Nat Hentoff	Aug. 4, 1969	do	1,250.00
	Oct. 13, 1969	do	1,250.00
	Oct. 22, 1969	Institutional funds	700.00
	Jan. 14, 1970	Student funds	1,500.00
Michael James	Jan. 9, 1969	do	300.00
	Mar. 12, 1970	Unknown	750.00
Carl Oglesby	Oct. 2, 1969	Institutional funds	1,250.00
Marcus Raskin	Mar. 21, 1969	do	800.00
	Feb. 19, 1970	Unknown	200.00
Richard Rothstein	Feb. 11, 1970	Student funds	830.00
Mark Rudd	Dec. 26, 1968	do	82.95
	Jan. 6, 1969	Unknown	100.00
	Feb. 2, 1969	Student funds	36.00
	Mar. 10, 1969	do	100.00
	Sept. 23, 1969	do	750.00
Robert Scheer	Sept. 24, 1969	Unknown	1,250.00
	Feb. 10, 1970	Student funds	1,200.00
	Feb. 12, 1970	Institutional funds	1,000.00
Mike Speigel	September 1968	do	Unknown
Reies Tijerina	Sept. 24, 1968	Unknown	Unknown
	May 21, 1969	do	Unknown
	May 1969	Student funds	500.00

Note: Total number of speakers 14; total number of speeches 32; total known amount paid to speakers $17,798.95; average honorarium per speech where amount known $711.95.

STUDENT NONVIOLENT COORDINATING COMMITTEE

Name	Date	Source of funds	Honorarium
Stokely Carmichael	Nov. 12, 1968	Unknown	Unknown
	November 1968	Student funds	$1,500

Note: Total number of speakers 1; total number of speeches 2; total known amount paid to speakers $1,500; average honorarium per speech where amount known $1,500.

YOUTH INTERNATIONAL PARTY

Name	Date	Source of funds	Honorarium
Abbie Hoffman	Apr. 22, 1969	Student funds	$750.00
	Mar. 30, 1970	Unknown	119.70
	Apr. 11, 1970	Student funds	2,000.00
	Apr. 13, 1970	Unknown	1,300.00
	May 5, 1970	Student funds	1,224.00
Paul Krassner	Dec. 9, 1969	Unknown	500.00
	Dec. 9, 1969	do	151.20
	Dec. 31, 1969	Student funds	25.00
Jerry Rubin	Jan. 7, 1969	do	300.00
	Apr. 6, 1970	do	500.00
	Apr. 10, 1970	Collection	Unknown
	May 5, 1970	Student funds	1,224.00
Nancy Rubin	Apr. 10, 1970	Collection	Unknown

Note: Total number of speakers 4; total number of speeches 13; total known amount paid to speakers $8,093.90; average honorarium per speech where amount known $622.76.

EPILOGUE

COMPOSITE—SPRING MOBE—NATIONAL MOBE AND NEW MOBILIZATION COMMITTEE TO END THE WAR IN VIETNAM

Name	Date	Source of funds	Honorarium
James Bevel	Nov. 12, 1968	Institutional funds	$200
	do	do	100
David Dellinger	May 5, 1970	Student funds	1,224
	May 15, 1970	Collection	Unknown
Douglas Dowd	May 7, 1970	Unknown	Unknown
Richard R. Fernandez	Nov. 15, 1969	Student funds	415
Carlton Goodlett	Oct. 1, 1968	Institutional funds	150
Dick Gregory	Sept. 19, 1968	Student funds	1,250
	Oct. 21, 1968	do	1,000
	Nov. 6, 1968	do	1,250
	Dec. 12, 1968	do	1,250
	Jan. 7, 1969	do	1,000
	Feb. 18, 1969	do	500
	Feb. 25, 1969	Institutional funds	1,250
	Oct. 9, 1969	Unknown	Unknown
	Oct. 30, 1969	do	900
	Dec. 10, 1969	do	Unknown
	February 1970	Student funds	1,250
	Feb. 4, 1970	do	1,250
	Feb. 5, 1970	do	1,000
	Feb. 17, 1970	do	1,000
	Mar. 5, 1970	None	None
	Mar. 8, 1970	Student funds	750
	Mar. 10, 1970	Institutional funds	1,000
	Mar. 20, 1970	Student funds ($500)	1,000
		Institutional funds ($500)	
	Apr. 16, 1970	Student funds	1,500
	Apr. 9, 1970	do	1,250
	July 23, 1970	Institutional funds	1,250
Deirdre Griswold	Oct. 22, 1969	Unknown	Unknown
Edward Keating	Nov. 20, 1969	Institutional funds	350
Staughton Lynd	Feb. 14, 1969	Student funds	900
	Oct. 15, 1969	Collection	Unknown
	Nov. 13, 1969	do	Unknown
Floyd McKissick	Mar. 12, 1969	Student funds	2,250
Steward Meacham	Dec. 6, 1968	do	70
Sidney Peck	Nov. 17, 1969	do	50
Mulford Q. Sibley	Jan. 28, 1969	do	100
Jerome Skolnick	Nov. 21, 1969	do	350
Benjamin Spock	Oct. 1, 1968	do	1,000
	Oct. 31, 1968	do	2,250
	Apr. 16, 1969	do	1,500
	Sept. 24, 1969	do	2,000
	Sept. 25, 1969	do	2,000
	Oct. 3, 1969	do	1,750
	Oct. 27, 1969	Institutional funds	2,000
	Jan. 23, 1970	Student funds	1,750
	Feb. 12, 1970	do	2,500
	Apr. 3, 1970	do	1,100
	Apr. 16, 1970	do	2,000
	Apr. 18, 1970	do	1,750

Note: Total number of speakers 15; total number of speeches 50; total known amount paid to speakers $47,409; average honorarium per speech where amount known $1,128.79.

Since, in a sampling from 3.8% of institutions of higher education, funds in this volume are derived by such persons, the Congress of the United States can reasonably conclude that the campus-speaking circuit is certainly the source of significant financing for members or supporters of organizations promoting disorderly, violent and revolutionary activity. Speaking appearances not only produce revenue but also afford a forum where the radicalization process may be continually expanded.

The Committee believes the limited sampling is sufficient to alert the Congress, college and university administrators, faculty, alumni, students, and parents to the probable extent of campus guest oratory in promoting the radical, revolutionary movement. A grave aspect of campus unrest and violence has been the personal injuries suffered and the serious damage to campus property following the extreme rhetoric of some speakers. If a speaker suggests propriety in killing public officials, or recommends destruction and violence as a desirable means of tearing down "the system" or "the establishment," there can, of course, be no *scientific certainty* that any killing, arson, bombing, or other violence which promptly follows was incited by him. It cannot be known in an *absolute degree*, excluding all doubts, that the overt criminal acts which ensue are the direct and proximate result of the rhetoric. But practical and reasonable persons know that such speech can be a contributing stimulant to such acts.

William Kunstler asserted at the University of Maryland on September 11, 1970, that he should be able to tell a crowd to burn an ROTC building. We cannot fail to note that the Isla Vista, California, branch of the Bank of America was burned by a mob on February 25, 1970, promptly after Kunstler told a crowd at a nearby University of California, Santa Barbara, "Every time I speak I mention the fact that I think people ought to be in the streets and some one says that's a fine thing for a lawyer to say, or it's not very legal to raise your fist in the air, but I say this to those critics, that the natural course in every civilization has been from routine protests to resistance and ultimately if resistance does not succeed, to revolution." Many others who have spoken on the Nation's campuses have uttered inflammatory rhetoric. The Constitutional guarantee of free speech has been broadly construed throughout our Nation's history, and wisely so, but inciting to riot or counseling the commission of a crime is properly a criminal offense and not constitutionally protected.

The extent of damage caused to a prime target of New Left rhetoricians—Reserve Officer Training Corps facilities on college and university campuses—is a matter of deep concern to Federal officials as well as to administrations of our schools of higher learning. During the last two academic years (1968–69, 1969–70), military authorities have recorded 307 incidents such as firebombing, theft, vandalism etc., ensuing from anti-ROTC activities which resulted in $1,471,875 total damage to property; $202,115 to Federal property; and $1,263,-760 to non-federal property. A primary objective of SDS was to drive ROTC off the campus. Overlooking the merits of an officer corps which is composed of men who are civilian oriented rather than career professionals, the New Left conjectured that it could fracture the American war effort in Vietnam, and perhaps America's total offensive capability, by forcing a discontinuance of ROTC and thereby depriving the military of the infusion of new officers.

SDS was repeatedly involved in ROTC disruptions. SDS's travelling orators preached the anti–ROTC message from campus to campus. A member of SDS in St. Louis, Michael Siskind, pleaded guilty on February 20, 1969 to attempted fire-bombing of the ROTC facility at Washington University. The multitudinous acts of violence directed toward such federal, or federally funded, programs and facilities have not occurred in a vacuum. It would require the most extreme and distorted reasoning to hold that they were all isolated incidents, unrelated to the generative forces unleashed by New Left organizational policies given widespread promulgation, acceptance and implementation by diverse forms of communication, including modern day circuit riders. These speakers with their well-worn theme, appearing on campus invited and uninvited, found ample numbers of students willing to listen. The number of serious incidents which have occurred strongly suggests that the messages were not totally ignored. (A heretofore unpublished report of ROTC damage resulting from acts of violence on campuses during the 1968–70 period covered by the report is printed as Appendix IV.)

Serious questions, some touching as well upon areas of responsibility of other committees, must yet be resolved: Do federal funds paid to institutions of higher learning enable the schools to give honoraria to speakers such as those identified in this report? Do these federal funds then add to the coffers of organizations intent upon violence to our democratic systems? Are changes warranted in the law to preclude such benefits? Are statutory measures necessary to insure greater safeguards for ROTC facilities and other federal property on campuses? Should the Congress re-examine the wisdom of utilizing institutions of higher learning for officer training, military recruitment, defense industry recruitment and defense research? These and other complex problems demand review by this and other concerned committees of Congress. They are not susceptible to simple solution. Additional facts in other areas must be developed, however, the data adduced should be relevant to analysis of the aforementioned legislative questions.

This scene shows part of the damage in the Rotunda of the U.S. Capitol on the Senate side, resulting from the explosion of a bomb planted in a washroom behind the cracked wall on the right March 1, 1971. Structural damage to the U.S. Capitol is estimated to run as high as $1 million.

Nationwide, there were 225 ordered evacuations of government buildings resulting from 773 bombing threats in 1970, which cost the government about $4.4 million in lost man hours, according to testimony before the House Subcommittee on Public Buildings and Grounds on March 10, 1971. Of 51 bombings of government buildings in only one instance have the bombers been apprehended. Some present and past government officials excused the bombings blaming them on the "immoral war in Vietnam."   U.P.I.

BIBLIOGRAPHY OF SUGGESTED READING

ACADEMIA IN ANARCHY — An Economic Diagnosis. James M. Buchanan and Nicos E. Devletoglou. Basic Books, Inc., New York, NY.

CONQUEST WITH WORDS. Roy E. Colby. Forward by Herbert A. Philbrick. Crestwood Books, Arlington, VA. 22202

DEMOCRACY IN AMERICA. Alexis de Tocqueville. Knopf, New York, NY.

FREEDOM AND FEDERALISM. Felix Morley. Regnery & Co., Chicago, IL.

HOW WE PROSPER UNDER FREEDOM. Warren T. Hackett. Epilogue by Dr. Emerson P. Schmidt, Citizens Evaluation Institute, 62 Ben Franklin, Washington, DC. 20044

LEFT OF LIBERAL. Anthony Bouscaren and Daniel Lyons, Crestwood Books, Arlington, Va. 22202

RELIGION AND CAPITALISM — ALLIES NOT ENEMIES. Edmund A. Opitz. Arlington House, New York, NY.

SOCIALISM. Ludwig Von Mises. Yale University Press, New Haven, CT.

TEACHERS OF DESTRUCTION. Alice Widener. Citizens Evaluation Institute, 62 Ben Franklin, Washington, DC. 20044

THE CHRISTIAN HISTORY OF THE CONSTITUTION. Verna M. Hall. The American Christian Constitution Press, San Francisco, CA.

THE COMMUNIST CONQUEST OF SHANGHAI. Dr. Paolo A. Rossi and Dr. Anthony Kubek. Twin Circle, NY and Crestwood Books, Arlington, VA. 22202

THE DIARY OF DAVID Q. LITTLE. R. Daniel McMichael. Arlington House, New York, NY.

THE FABIAN FREEWAY. Rose L. Martin. Fidelis Publishers, Inc., Santa Monica, CA.

THE FAILURE OF THE "NEW ECONOMICS". Henry Hazlitt. Van Nostrand Publishing Co., New York, NY.

THE FREEMAN. (Journal). Foundation for Economic Education. Irvington, NY.

THE LID: 50 Years of Democratic Education. Mena Weisenberg. League for Industrial Democracy, New York, NY.

THE MORAL ALTERNATIVE TO SOCIALISM. Irving E. Howard. Citizens Evaluation Institute, 62 Ben Franklin, Washington, DC. 20044

THE POLITICS OF SURRENDER. Stanton Evans. Devin-Adair, New York, NY.

THE PROTESTANT REVOLT. Dr. James DeForest Murch. Crestwood Books, Arlington, VA. 22202

THE ROAD TO SERFDOM. F.A. Hayek, University of Chicago Press, Chicago, IL.

THE STORY OF THE LAW. Renế A. Wormser. Simon & Schuster, New York, NY.

THE TRUTH ABOUT BOULWARISM — Trying To Do Right Voluntarily. Lemuel R. Boulware. Bureau of National Affairs, Inc., Washington, DC.

WITNESS. Whittaker Chambers. Random House, New York, NY.

WORKERS PARADISE LOST. Eugene Lyons. Funk and Wagnalls, New York, NY.

CRESTWOOD BOOKS, Inc. Distributor
P.O. Box 2096, Arlington, Va. 22202

Kindly rush the following number of copies of books checked.

REVOLUTIONARY ACTIONS . . . U.S.A. . . . *In Retrospect* - What To Do Now, compiled by Bruce Alger, including a DICTIONARY OF DOUBLE TALK by Roy E. Colby.

(   ) Single copy $1.50; (   ) 3 for $4; (   ) 5 for $6.

TEACHERS OF DESTRUCTION by Alice Widener.

(   ) Single copy $3; (   ) 3 for $8; (   ) 5 for $13.

BOTH of the above books -

(   ) $4.50; (   ) 3 of both for $11.50; (   ) 5 of both for $18.

HOW WE PROSPER UNDER FREEDOM, a "short course" in Free-Choice Economics, by W.T. Hackett and Dr. Emerson P. Schmidt.

(   ) Single copy $2.25; (   ) 3 for $5.

Payment of $____ is enclosed. My check is made payable to CITIZENS EVALUATION INSTITUTE. I understand you pay shipping charges when payment is enclosed. Write for other quantity prices.

NAME_____
Please Print

NAME OF COMPANY_____

ADDRESS_____

CITY_____

STATE_____ ZIP_____

If you wish books sent to your list, simply add to the multiple copy price, 24¢ per copy for REVOLUTIONARY ACTIONS . . . U.S.A. . . . *In Retrospect* - What To Do Now; 35¢ each for TEACHERS OF DESTRUCTION (or 40¢ for both); and 24¢ each for HOW WE PROSPER UNDER FREEDOM. These charges pay for addressing, handling, packaging, postage and shipping. (Please include Zip codes in your list.) Extra charge for Special Handling.

The CITIZENS EVALUATION INSTITUTE, sponsor and publisher of REVOLUTIONARY ACTIONS. . . U.S.A. . . . In Retrospect - What To Do Now (including a DICTIONARY OF DOUBLE TALK); TEACHERS OF DESTRUCTION; and HOW WE PROSPER UNDER FREEDOM, has arranged with Crestwood Books, Inc. to be the distributor for them. Send orders directly to Crestwood for fast service but make checks payable to CITIZENS EVALUATION INSTITUTE.

THE CITIZENS EVALUATION INSTITUTE

is a non-profit educational corporation. For further information write:

CITIZENS EVALUATION INSTITUTE
62 Ben Franklin
Washington, D.C. 20044

51990

10-300